PETER BRAITHWAITE
STUDIO

NATURAL FORCES
DESIGN & CRAFT OF A NOVA SCOTIAN
ARCHITECTURAL IDENTITY

PETER BRAITHWAITE
STUDIO

NATURAL FORCES
DESIGN & CRAFT OF A NOVA SCOTIAN
ARCHITECTURAL IDENTITY

Foreword by Aaron Betsky
Introduction & Interview by James McCown
Essays by Peter Braithwaite and Brian Carter
Principal Photography by Ema Peter
Visualizations by Yurii Suhov
Edited by Oscar Riera Ojeda

OSCAR RIERA OJEDA
PUBLISHERS

For mom, dad,
Emily and our boys.

P.B.

Contents

Acknowledgements

by Peter Braithwaite

At the onset of this project, the notion of crafting a paper artifact that would embody the contributions of innumerable individuals over a ten-year period seemed daunting. Through the guidance of my capable collaborators this project gradually developed and eventually found its final form. This process expressed the similarity between the creation of a book and the crafting of a building. Both require flexibility, intense rigour, and the persistent pursuit of clarity. I would like to acknowledge all the people that made this process successful and enjoyable.

First and foremost, I would like to thank our PBS team, both past and present. Your tireless endurance and detailed focus throughout the years have ensured our projects were developed with the care and craft they deserved. Our novel approach to practice requires diligent, versatile, and creative individuals. We have been extremely lucky in this regard.

I would like to thank Aaron Betsky, Brian Carter and James McCown for your insightful contributions. It is not often I can step outside my daily activities and reflect on our work. Doing so with such an esteemed group of individuals was a pleasure. Thanks to Oscar Riera Ojeda and Florencia Damilano whose ongoing commitment to the craft of bookmaking brought this project to life.

Much of our firm's success is owed to the clients that placed trust in our firm, especially those that did so before we had a substantial portfolio of built work. I hold dearly the friendships that have been forged through our shared interest in creating.

My deepest gratitude is extended to my wife, Emily, for her endless encouragement and support. I would also like to thank my lifelong friends, who have played the most pivotal role in shaping the person I am today: Craig, Cory, Darren, Dave, Dennis, Greg, Jo, Ken, Marco, and Matt. Thanks to Ben for your boundless enthusiasm and limitless rigour in the early days of our company, you are dearly missed.

My biggest thanks are reserved for my mom and dad, I have no words for all you have provided me.

Foreword

by Aaron Betsky

Peter Braithwaite's Black Magic

Peter Braithwaite's buildings are mostly black. Sometimes they are dark gray, but that does not diminish their presence in the windswept landscape of Nova Scotia in which they arise. Closing themselves off from the elements and appearing as abstractions of otherwise familiar houses, they stand like strangely familiar enigmas. That their insides are simple and airy spaces slathered in wood makes their combination of slight weirdness and common sense typicality even odder. Their beauty comes from their ability, as time and those winds weather them and their sense of rightness in their landscape stands forth, to become essential Novia Scotia buildings.

The working compound Braithwaite built for himself in the village of Terence Bay, Nova Scotia, typifies his architecture. The main component of a sparsely built development of mainly vacation homes is a rectangular tube floating over the rocks and scree on an elevated site set back from the bay. Like most of the architect's buildings, the structure barely touches the land, instead establishing its form as separate from its surroundings. Clad in wood stained to a dark color, the studio opens up at either end with expanses of glass, the back of which lets you see the building's interior workings, while the front provides a view out to the ocean. A continuous strip of glass also interrupts the vertical siding on the side from which you approach, allowing those inside to view out while they are at their desks. Inside, six engineered timber frames keep the front of the space completely open, leaving the service space to tuck into two levels at the rear. On the inside as well, wood sets the tone, dominating the main room in the form of bookcases and wood walls.

The compound's workshop consists of two pavilions with eccentrically angled shed roofs. They are a bar cut in two, shaped to recall the local vernacular, and placed directly on the land. These more utilitarian structures are faced partially in black standing seam metal and partially in the same gray wood as the studio, interrupted by large openings that provide light for the woodworking areas.

Down the hill from these structures, an A-frame building, started as a student design/build project at Dalhousie University, where Braithwaite teaches, and continued by him as an architect, provides a single volume of space, completely clad in wood on its long ends and inside. This structure is not split, but kinked in the middle to respond to the slope on which it sits and over which one end protrudes and seems to float over the tumbling rocks. The interior provides a double-height living area with services again tucked into one end.

These three (or four) buildings are examples of the forms Braithwaite likes to use: rectangular objects, sometimes with off-kilter shed or hipped roofs, either raised off the ground for views and so as not to interrupt the site, sliced or kinked when they get to be too long for comfort or compositional logic, clad in dark wood or metal in a vertical pattern, with interiors that are simple and show off as much of the structure as the architect can manage. They are straightforward, but never simple, playing off their locations with angles, cuts, and contortions that specify their abstraction to site and use.

Peter Braithwaite developed this working method in response to the location in which almost all of his work is located, the peninsula of Nova Scotia that sticks out into the Atlantic Ocean with a low-lying and sparsely vegetated spread of rocks, scree, forests, and other low vegetation hugging the countless inlets, bays, fjords, and rises that make up the territory. On that landscape, the settlers who displaced the First Nations inhabitants built dwellings and other structures as isolated, usually wood-framed and -clad objects sitting tautly and with an erect posture on the land – you will see no huddling into closely set rows or spreading out over the landscape in the manner of either their English or Shingle Style American cousins. As the economy of fishing and hardscrabble agriculture transformed into one focused on service industries and tourism, these types became inspiration for objects meant to enjoy the landscape, rather than use its resources. It is such vacation and weekend homes that have become Braithwaite's specialty.

The architect who developed a working method and formal language on which both Braithwaite and the other notable residential architect in contemporary Nova Scotia, Omar Gandhi, draw, and for whom both of these designers worked, is Brian MacKay-Lyons. A native son who trained both in Halifax, Nova Scotia, and at the University of California in Los Angeles with Charles Moore, MacKay-Lyons used his education in the Postmodern reacceptance of historical styles and vernacular forms, as well as his deep knowledge of his home, to develop a domestic architecture that responds to its settings with often sculptural and expressive abstractions of those traditions and places.

Braithwaite readily acknowledges MacKay-Lyons' influence on his architecture: he studied with him and was his employee before collaborating with Gandhi, who also worked in the MacKay-Lyons office, and then setting up his own office. Sometimes the dominance of the elder architect can be a hindrance, as when Braithwaite admits that he feels he has to avoid certain forms or plan arrangements out of fear that MacKay-Lyons "owns" them, but he also clearly develops some of his language, material palette, and working method out of his experience at MacKay-Lyons Sweetapple firm. When I went to visit Braithwaite to see what he had designed and built, the first place he took me was a village in which MacKay-Lyons had designed almost all the structures.

Other aspects of his background and experience have also formed Braithwaite as an architect. Born in an agricultural town in Ontario, Canada, near Detroit, to veterinarian and scientist parents, he initially studied biology at the University of British Columbia in Vancouver before switching to fine arts with a concentration on photography. He developed his high school experience working in a lumberyard into a career as a carpenter before deciding that architecture would be the perfect combination of science, art, and making. Having made his decision late, the only school he could attend was Dalhousie in Halifax, where he not only encountered MacKay-Lyons and the thriving architecture culture the elder teacher and designer had created, but also his future wife and a community he made his own. For Braithwaite, who is currently pursuing a Ph.D. that seeks to combine the knowledge of a given landscape available through architecture and environmental sciences, the ability to see, document, analyze, and then restructure the place he now calls home is central to his pursuits as a professional.

That place is shaped not only by its climate and geology, but also by the wood culture of shipbuilding and the particular aesthetic and building methodology mixing British, Scottish, French Acadian, and American influences into shapes whose timber technology and isolated stance, though somewhat submerged in the Province's major city, Halifax, is still evident in all of the exurban sites where Braithwaite works. His decision to establish his office in Terence Bay (though he has since moved back to Halifax to be near not only clients and workers, but also his family and now rents the compound out on Airbnb) gave him the chance to develop his own response to these traditions, influences, and sites. The architect has embraced the roughness and strangeness of this relatively isolated place, giving it shape in his dark forms.

Braithwaite also largely builds his own homes. He has collected a group of craftspeople around him that can further his own knowledge of and experience in wood craft, housing them in a second purpose-built workshop in Halifax's harbor. The crew can do almost all the major work on the houses themselves, and Braithwaite has developed techniques for joining, staining, and structuring work that is particular to both locally available materials and expertise and to the forms that he has developed through his ten years of practice. His signature dark gray and black stains are part of that repertoire, as are the ways in which he manipulates rolls of standing seam metal siding, rather than using pre-cut pieces. As a result, the buildings have a sense of tightness in their dark presence, but also a way in which they respond, but also give back a different palette, to the buildings around them. In his studio office, Braithwaite then develops the variations of the compositional elements he has also developed over his years of work in wood models, all of the same scale, that let him study the spatial relationship of each commission in detail.

The resulting work is, even when not a compound of forms, usually compound in its form. Nearby his former studio, for instance, he has designed two small cabins on a deck that you reach by rising up along a gentle raised wood walkway and stairs. Perched high enough to catch a view of the distant ocean, these gray-stained rectangles sprout canted roofs separated from the siding with clerestory windows. They are placed not quite next to each other, allowing the space to rotate around them. Clad almost completely in wood and plywood on the inside, they give room, respectively, to living in a two-story high space and compact bedroom areas for a small family visiting here on weekends and summers. Rising high above the spread of the seashore landscape, these Lambkill Ridge Cottages, as Braithwaite calls them, sit on their site as lightly as he could manage, even if that means exposing much of their more prosaic underside and services – an issue with much of the architect's work. What matters more to him is the manner in which they compact human occupation into a tight form that stands up to its geology and weather, sheltering its inhabitants with beautifully detailed paneling and exposed structural members.

Currently, Braithwaite is experimenting with extending the ways in which such minimal structures can occupy the almost always gently rolling Nova Scotia landscape. Thus he has a scheme for three double height boxes that can stand near his property in Terence Bay. Each of these flat-roofed, stilt-standing Rocky Rock Cabins would consist of a single space, its structure and siding exposed on the inside and clad with vertical wood siding, with the service areas tucked into the rear in a compacted and yet enlarged version

Back Bay Studio.

Back Bay Shops detail.

Lambkill Ridge Cottage under construction.

of one of the Lambkill Ridge pavilions. The idea would be to make these cottages available for rental.

He is also experimenting with simple versions of the A-frame, including in the Attic Lofts, versions of the experiment he built next to his former studio. Perched in Nova Scotia's wine country, these kinked, triangular structures would also serve as rentable rooms. The nearby B Loft, meanwhile, is a single A-frame room lifted off the ground and bisected by a concrete tower that would provide access and services.

Braithwaite's work continually oscillates between such compaction, which seems to be his preference, and an extension demanded by function and views, often in the same commission. He builds his forms up out of geometric elements that key into each other and the land, while lifting the structure off the ground to gather its various shapes and spaces under roofs that often extend beyond the main mass. Yet he also likes to split his buildings, as in the former workshop, and even make them into completely separate buildings, as in the Lambkill Ridge Cottage. There he opens up the masses to entrance and views and extends the landscape between them.

A highly controlled representation of this tension is the house and dual studio Braithwaite designed at Nova Scotia's northern tip for an artist couple. Called either Caribou Point Studio or, more descriptively, Meet in the Middle House, it consists of one, very long object split in the middle by what in the U.S. is called a "dog trot": a porch in the middle of the house over which the roof continues. That interruption is the point of entry into the House's living area, while also providing a view to the bay and ocean beyond.

Programmatically, the House stretches between the his-and-hers studios at either end, which provide the two artists with quiet and private working areas. In-between is the open living area and a bedroom. As in almost all of Braithwaite's houses, these spaces are simple and compact, eschewing either formal complication or elaborate fixtures in favor of the expression of structure and wood (although most of the rooms here are simply finished with white-painted walls and ceilings) and, in this case, the eccentrically pitched ceiling.

A secondary building housing a garage and guest apartment turns the House into a compound, framing the approach and deferring to the back meadow that slopes down towards the coastline. The roof pulls up tight and vertical from the front and then slopes more gently towards the fall of the land and the view. Unusually for Braithwaite's structures and to underline both the House's and the site's reach, the buildings are clad with the usual, dark stained wood, but here running horizontally. The black-painted standing seam metal roof then caps and contains the run of living spaces below it.

In smaller structures Braithwaite has designed, he prefers to turn his buildings into collages of pitched, gabled and flat-roofed elements fitting into each other. Seabright, for instance, a house tucked away along a stream and pond in the middle of a forest, snuggles under a single slanted roof that cantilevers over the entrance area. While the roof marks and extends the living area below, added rooms are expressed in vertically sided wood saddlebags attached to them. The whole composition fits tightly onto its site, containing all functions in less than a thousand square feet, while opening up to views of its idyllic location.

Braithwaite is gravitating increasingly towards such expressive and dominating roof structures to mark the major living areas as well as the presence of the house as a whole. In earlier designs, however, he also created flat-roofed boxes that confront their ocean views with a clearly human-made artifact. The Sandbox is the most extreme of such structures: a two story box that resembles the former studio turned on its end. The side facing the rear approach is almost completely closed, with only a Corten steel U-shape framing the entrance door and a window on the floor above it. The architect mirrored that entrance marker's rough, metallic presence with an exterior staircase that starts on the side of the second story and leads up to a roof deck.

On the beach side, the box opens up with two lines of windows, each of which wrap around opposite corners to further break down a mass that is considerably taller than that of its neighbors. Inside, the spaces are unusually simple in their finishes for Braithwaite's practice, consisting of white shells in which the views are the main point.

While these houses stay back from the often violent ocean, many of Braithwaite's recent clients seem to want to tempt the elements by building as close to the waves as possible. In the tk House, the structure is designed to confront the fact that the waves might in fact enter directly onto its territory by raising the main structure off the ground, anchored to one side by a concrete base that also houses the client's main water storage cisterns. The house itself consists of two parallel gabled bars, the front one containing the living room and facing the ocean, and the rear one opening up to the living areas. Both forms are clad with a (black) metal siding that can withstand the weather, while windows carved into the front piece allow for expansive views.

The conjoining of two major elements with a smaller connective device is an organizational principle Braithwaite has used in several of his houses as an alternative to the split configuration of the designs described above. Here he is able to create more compact buildings that express their major functional spaces, usually with gabled or hipped roofs beneath which the long sides are relatively closed, while the ends are open to views, and the service functions, such as bathrooms and utilities, although sometimes also the entrance area, nestle between these two elements.

The Twilight House, currently under construction near his former studio in Terence Bay, is a particularly strong version of this composition. It consists of two eccentrically hipped forms that spread out from chimneys that anchor the house to the ground. The two bars slip by each other, while their roofs' long directions run in opposite directions, both breaking up the building mass and concentrating it on the area at the small bar that connects them. The arrangement also offers different views from the living areas in the front-facing structure and the bedrooms in rear one.

A much larger version of this arrangement is that of one of Braithwaite's few designs for a site far away from Novia Scotia. The Armstrong Island House occupies the collection of rocks and soil that goes by that name in Jack's Lake, which is part of the "cottage area" north of Toronto. Although the landscape is roughly similar to the one in which the architect is used to working, it is more densely forested and his design is here surrounded by rather more placid water than that he is used to confronting.

The Armstrong Island building is also much larger than most of Braithwaite's other buildings, although not nearly of the scale of some of the "cottages" nearby. The two hipped roofs that define the House's two major wings are again are eccentric, spreading out from

the core towards the views of the lake, but they are also splayed from each other at right angles on the high ridge at the Island's center. These caps also continue, in a manner Braithwaite likes to achieve when he can, in long cantilevers to shelter porches at the bar's ends, while the bar containing the living area is much more open than those of the architect's houses that hunker down in their landscape.

Lifted above the landscape, the Armstrong Island House tries to live as lightly on the land as possible, including by drawing its own water, incinerating human waste, and gaining power from solar cells. Those systems serve spaces that are as large as the client's means and taste, clad largely in wood and showing off the timber elements that make the rooms possible. Unlike the Nova Scotia buildings, Braithwaite did not build this structure with his own crew of carpenters and construction experts, but relied on local craftspeople who were able to achieve some of the same levels of detailing and finish.

Almost all of Peter Braithwaite's commissions have been for houses in Nova Scotia's open landscape, however. Although he started with a few commercial commissions and has designed his own offices and workshop, he does not consider them representative of what he is trying to achieve with his work. That does not mean he lacks the ambition to design larger commercial or institutional structures, and some of the most intriguing of the many models that populate his studio represent designs for schools and arts buildings.

A hint of how Braithwaite might address more urban context is available in one of his larger commissions, the Armcrest Road House. Situated in a suburban neighborhood, the house is a gabled form (which of course is asymmetrical and black) clad in wood. Its mass abstracts and jumps up the scale of the Colonial and Tudor homes around it, gathering the windows into long lines and raising the roof up considerably above the neighbors' structures. One part of the House extends forward to break down this large mass, while a chimney nails down its side. To the rear, that extension is mirrored with a second floor bedroom block that cantilevers over the windows of the living area below.

Inside, Braithwaite found space for a family that consists of six people in rooms that are generous, but, as in all his other houses, not elaborately shaped. They also combine the roughness that comes from exposed ceiling joists with exquisitely worked handrails, screens, and cabinetry produced in the architect's own shop. This is obviously the home of a client with means, but also one that wants to fit within and extend the kind of culture that has shaped Halifax and Nova Scotia.

That is what Peter Braithwaite is seeking to do in most of his commissions. He combines an attention to wood detailing with simple planes, and layers complex saddlebags, extensions, cantilevers and even complete separations onto buildings that, in the end, are relatively forthright in their final form. That is true both on the outside, where the gray or black materiality further tones down the structures while also emphasizing their otherness from the landscape, and on the inside, where the architect eschews expressive ceilings or spatial penetrations in favor of functional rooms. By now, Braithwaite knows how to put structures together with great skill, and we can only hope that he will be able to extend his commissions to address a larger and more public form of architecture. Nova Scotia – and other places – could use a bit more of this black beauty.

Aaron Betsky

Introduction

by James McCown

"Everything in Nova Scotia is touched by the sea, which finds its way into our food and drink, the way our skin feels, how we talk and smell, the roll of our gait and even how we look at the world."

— John Demont, *The Long Way Home: A Personal History of Nova Scotia*

Nova Scotia and the northern Atlantic Ocean exist in a tense détente, the former always aware that the latter's fury might be unleashed at any moment. Architect Peter Braithwaite respects and designs to this dichotomy, creating waterfront homes with an eye toward resiliency, their concrete and steel support pilings a strong bulwark against the raging surf.

Braithwaite is more than an architect. He is also a craftsman and woodworker and these allied talents have served him well as he has built his practice. His range of clients is as varied as his buildings – some for wealthy patrons but the vast majority are custom single-family homes for people of modest means. The architect is entrusted with their life's savings and recognizes the responsibility that comes with this fiduciary role.

Braithwaite was confronted in childhood by extremes: On the one hand his residency in Windsor, Ontario, just across a strait from Detroit, a city that holds a long-time fascination for him. Sojourns in British Columbia and Ontario eventually took him to Halifax, where he studied at Dalhousie University, founded in 1818. (In 1997 Dalhousie merged with TUNS, Technical University of Nova Scotia.)

What concrete is to brutalist modernism and stucco is to the American southwest, wood is to Nova Scotia. It is a natural choice for a province of one of the world's largest countries with unfathomable amounts of woodlands. But Braithwaite, as much as he uses wood, argues that it is not possible to take advantage of recent advances in engineered lumber construction types: "The supply chain just isn't there yet" in Atlantic Canada.

"Atlantic Canada has a deep-seated connection to light timber frame construction that is strongly intertwined with the culture of this place, in a sort of inseparable way," Braithwaite says.

The sea and wood are inexorably connected in Nova Scotia. The poet Elizabeth Bishop, who grew up in the province, wrote in her poem "The Monument":

> It is an artifact of wood
> Wood holds together better than sea or
> cloud . . . It is the beginning of a painting, a piece of
> sculpture, a poem, or monument,
> and all of wood. Watch it closely.

Wood is used at all stages of a project. In Braithwaite's downtown Halifax studio one sees architectural models mounted on exquisite topographic surfaces of wood, polished to a smoothness and high sheen. They are a feast for the eye and the hand.

Examples of Braithwaite's waterfront sensibility abound. Of the Back Bay Studio in Terrence Bay, he writes: "Inspired by local building practices, the cladding of the exterior is composed of locally sourced Hemlock boards which enables the exterior of the studio to age naturally and withstand the harsh Atlantic climate."

Salsman Cottage.

The Black Point Residence elicits this response: "Located along Northumberland Strait in Black Point, Nova Scotia, the building's form is comprised of three distinct geometric volumes which each comprise specific programmatic functions. The two gable structures have specific programmatic roles in that one is dedicated to shared living and gathering spaces while the other is dedicated to sleeping and bathing." The third rectilinear volume intersects and skewers both gables and contains the building's circulation and services spaces.

Of the Armcrescent Residence in Halifax, a more urban intervention, he states: "This residence represents a new opportunity for multi-generational or blended family dwelling within one structure rather than breaking down a family unit to accommodate the established archetypes found within the neighborhood."

Corten and other weathered steel products are additional choices in the architect's materials repertoire. The Sandbox, in neighboring New Brunswick, boasts a wrap-around steel staircase. Braithwaite explains: "The exterior expression of the building features eastern white cedar and weathering steel that will allow the building's facades to age with grace and in time seamlessly blend within the weathered landscape."

As a proponent of the triad of design, craftsmanship and building, Braithwaite's practice is, if not unique, clearly out of the ordinary. He recognizes instinctively the imperative of sustainability, and nowhere is this more keenly felt than in the former British colonies of Canada and Australia, the latter home to Glenn Murcutt, Braithwaite's favorite architect. Both lands are vast and sparsely populated. Perhaps from these crucibles emerges a particular appreciation of the architect's influence on the earth.

Part of this sensitivity to materials is an appreciation and celebration of how they weather. "In Atlantic Canada, the building you do today will look different tomorrow," Braithwaite says. "The act of nature and weathering and the harsh environment on structures is so apparent. We tell our client that the cladding is going to weather immediately, we're going to have gray weathered shingles."

"As you drive around these areas, you can't help but notice the windswept nature of all the buildings. That was immediately apparent to me in Nova Scotia. This is one of the reasons I love this place, its modest, rugged nature."

Braithwaite's explorations have taken him far afield from the bucolic place he now calls home. "When I was studying Detroit, I read the book *The Necessity for Ruins, and Other Topics*, by John Brinckerhoff Jackson; and *On Weathering: The Life of Buildings in Time*, by Mohsen Mostafavi and David Leatherbarrow. These helped me solidify the notion that you can't design for the moment. You must design for time. Will the building change programs? Will it change into something else in a few years?"

"I think the ruins of Detroit and the rugged nature of Canada's East Coast aligned in the sense that they show how weather acts on buildings over time. It's always been of interest to me. I've always liked abandoned warehouses and forsaken churches. There's something captivating about them."

As a design/build firm, Braithwaite's studio is responsible for the entire creation of the building, from the time the initial sketches are done until the time the client moves in. Rooted in the Middle Ages, when the "master builder" (the architect) was also the "master constructor," this method of project delivery allows the architect to design with the totality of the building process in mind.

"In the traditional design/bid/build scenario. there is an exclusion of the builder's voice," Braithwaite says. "The entire design process moves toward when the construction drawings are ready to go, at which point your builder is seeing the drawings the first time, when the design is fully baked. Any change from that point results in expensive and time-consuming charge orders. They require redrawing on the architect's part, possibly redrawing on the engineer's part. And there's a cost that a builder will charge for any change that's outside of the drawings that he's bid on."

Braithwaite continues: "Our argument is that from the get-go, our building team is integrated with our architecture team. So we're designing something where there's no surprises. In this way our building team knows how to construct everything we're designing. We find this cuts down on the adversarial relationship among the builder, the client, and the owner."

This all-encompassing vision of the building arts calls to mind legendary ateliers in the early part of the 20th century – The Bauhaus, the Wiener Werkstätte, Frank Lloyd Wright's Taliesin and so on. Braithwaite's architectural stance yields structures that begin life as exquisite wood models and morph into carefully crafted abodes with custom cabinetry and built-in seating. He oversees every detail, from start to finish.

The demanding environment of Atlantic Canada requires nothing less. For the waterfront house, the ocean's fury is met with carefully crafted roofs and siding that hold nature at bay, at least for now. And yet always there are the forces of Neptune, a constant reminder of architects' allied responsibility to design with nature while remaining in awe of its raw and merciless power.

Built Projects

BACK BAY STUDIO

Location: Terence Bay, Nova Scotia, Canada

Situated along a rocky outcrop that overlooks the Atlantic Ocean, the Back Bay Studio is sited within the culturally rich community of Terence Bay. This small fishing community, located along Nova Scotia's eastern shore, is made up of rocky cliff faces and rolling hillsides that extend down to the ocean's edge.

The architectural form of the building is driven by a desire to frame the coastal landscape and respect the sensitive ecosystem that exists on the site. The procession through the studio invites the user from the entry into a double height volume that captures the dramatic coastal landscape as it winds down to the banks of Back Bay. The east and west walls of the studio were designed to work together to both capture panoramic views over the barren landscape but also take advantage of natural cross ventilation. The overarching connection to the surrounding landscape felt throughout the building reinforces our firm's commitment to create architecture that directly engages with the natural environment.

The bold expression of structure throughout the building presented an opportunity to integrate design and craftsmanship. The six large engineered timber rigid frames that make up the superstructure of the building create a rhythmic motif throughout the building and clearly define the spatial division of the interior program. Also, as the firm continues to grow, this structural strategy allows the interior to be adjusted to meet the company's changing needs. Inspired by local building practices, the cladding of the exterior is composed of locally sourced Hemlock boards which enables the exterior of the studio to age naturally and withstand the harsh Atlantic climate.

Back Bay Studio provided a great opportunity to feature the integrated approach of the firm's design and construction teams. It also gives prospective clients the ability to experience a built project that expresses the quality of craftsmanship and design ethos of the practice.

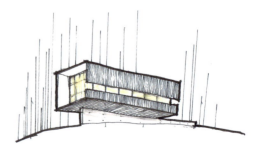

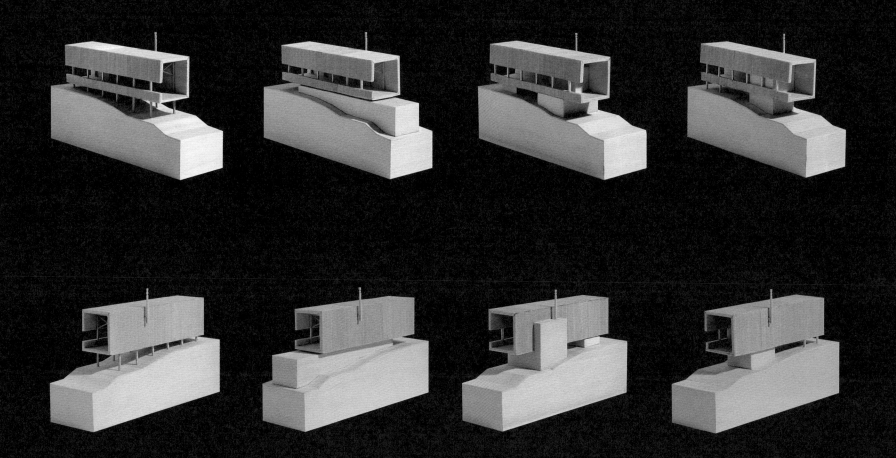

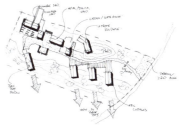

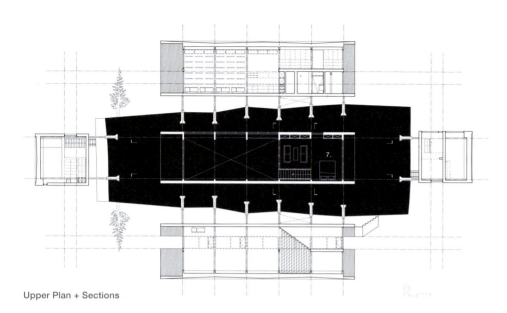

Upper Plan + Sections

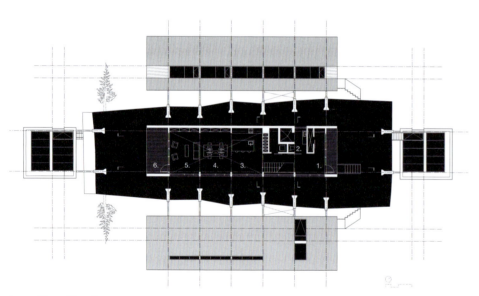

Lower Plan + Elevations

1. Entry
2. Bath
3. Kitchen +
   Dining Room
4. Studio
5. Living Room
6. Patio
7. Bedroom

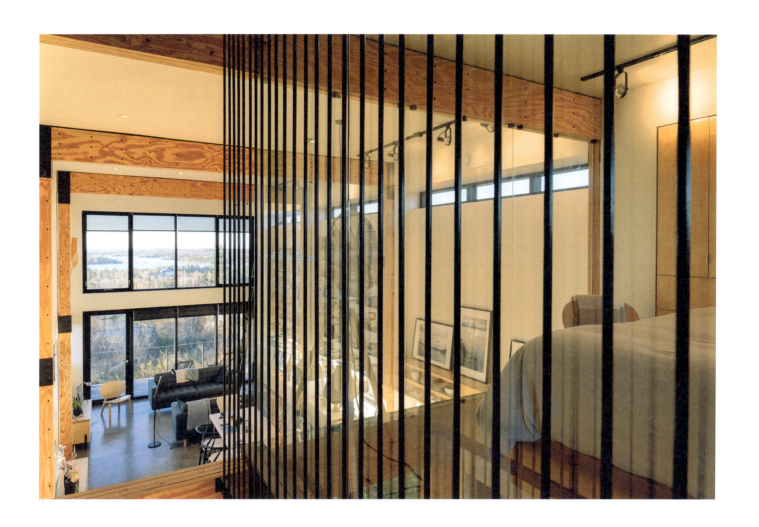

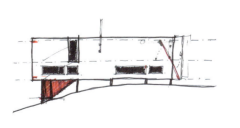

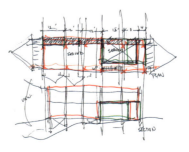

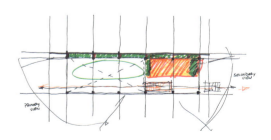

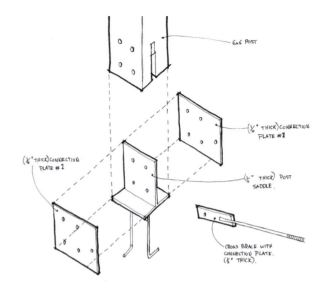

6x6 POST

($\frac{1}{4}$" THICK) CONNECTION PLATE #1

($\frac{1}{4}$" THICK) CONNECTION PLATE # 2

($\frac{1}{2}$" THICK) POST SADDLE.

CROSS BRACE WITH CONNECTION PLATE. ($\frac{1}{4}$" THICK).

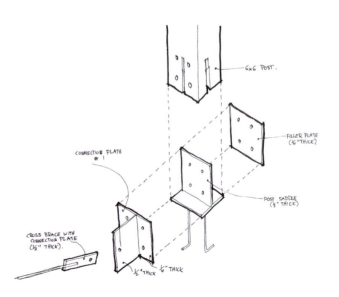

6x6 POST.

CONNECTION PLATE # 1

FILLER PLATE ($\frac{1}{8}$" THICK)

POST SADDLE ($\frac{1}{2}$" THICK)

CROSS BRACE WITH CONNECTION PLATE ($\frac{1}{8}$" THICK).

$\frac{1}{2}$" THICK $\frac{1}{4}$" THICK

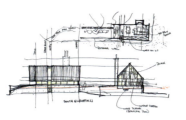

Guest House Sketches

THE SANDBOX

Location: Bathurst, New Brunswick, Canada

The site presented horizontal driving rain and harsh southeastern winds upon our first visit which gave our design team a keen awareness of the extreme weather that the Gulf of St. Lawrence could offer. After a very brief introduction to our new client, we were invited to find cover within the harshly weathered seasonal cottage that previously existed on the site. This strongly weathered structure gave further insight into the dramatic climatic conditions of this location along Bay of Chaleur in Bathurst, New Brunswick.

Although the existing humble cottage showed signs of seasonal abuse with torn window screens, patched plywood floors, and windows that no longer kept the water out, the reason for the building's siting was abundantly clear. The long stretching beach in both directions along the shore of the bay coupled with an unimpeded view out to the open ocean generated an overwhelming sense of awe. The location was ruggedly beautiful, and the clients' proposed ambitions seemed both appropriate to the waterfront location and challenging enough to pique our interest. It was immediately clear that connecting the extensive coastal landscape to domestic activities was going to be the driving force of this project design.

The datums of the windows were carefully considered to ensure a comfortable and purposeful connection from the dwelling spaces to the natural landscape. An awareness of the relationship of the natural environment to the domestic activities of the dwelling were of utmost importance.

The main living area provides panoramic views to the ocean through large, glazed windows which wrap the corners of the space and flood the room with warm morning light. The client's passion for gathering and food preparation inspired the kitchen to be organized around a custom island that acts as the central hearth of the room. Above the kitchen and living area, the master bedroom displays views of the mouth of the bay through another corner wrapped window.

Stacking the sleeping spaces on top of the living spaces allowed a rooftop patio with elevated views above the single-story neighboring cottages as well as views down the long stretching beach. The form of the building, "the box," was a result of the decision to access the rooftop and in turn resulted in the rectilinear elevations of the building.

Being aware of the harsh Atlantic climate, our team selected cladding materials and assemblies that matched the local building culture and costruction practices. The exterior expression of the building features eastern white cedar and Corten steel that will allow the building's facades to age with grace and in time seamlessly blend within the weathered landscape.

Designed around the lifestyle of a young industrious couple in New Brunswick, The Sandbox was realized by celebrating community. Designed and built on a very humble budget, local connections to regional trades and manufacturers fostered lasting relationships between the architect, the client and community members that resulted in an elegant, well-crafted dwelling that will stand the tests of time.

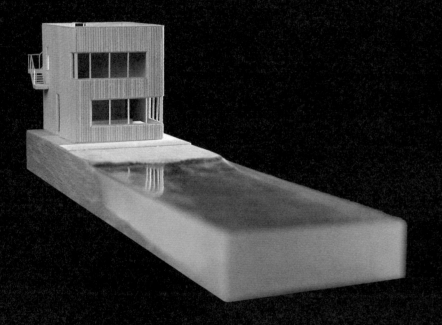
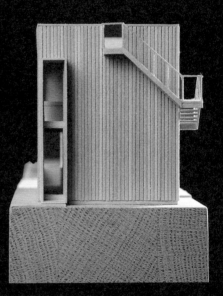

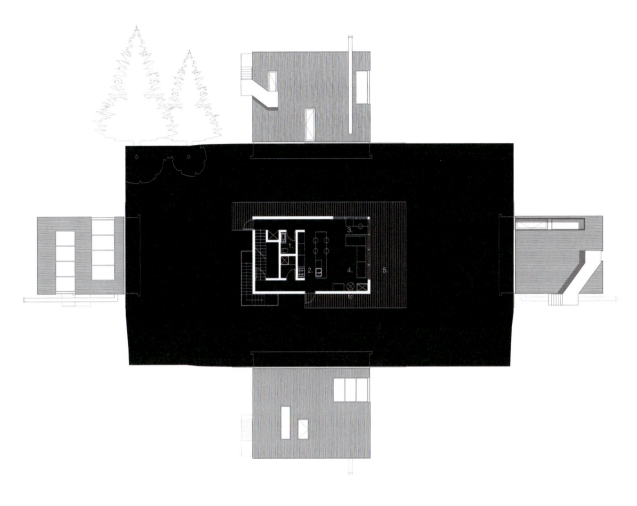

Plan

1. Bath
2. Kitchen + Dining Room
3. Study
4. Living Room
5. Patio

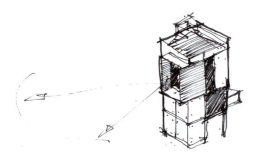

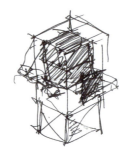

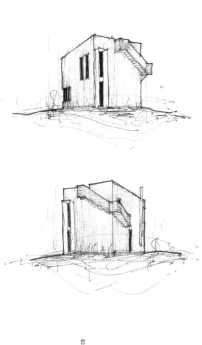

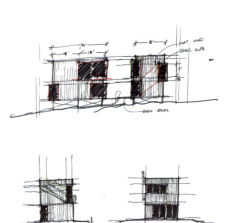

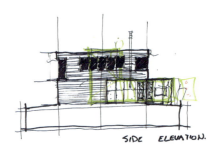

SIDE ELEVATION.

SEABRIGHT RESIDENCE

Location: Seabright, Nova Scotia, Canada

Located in the small coastal community of Seabright, Nova Scotia, this private residence overlooks a picturesque lake that is connected to the ocean by a tidal brook. Building upon Nova Scotia's rich wood culture, this modest 1000 square foot house is entirely constructed form locally sourced wood products.

Much of the early schematic design work for this residence explored visual, tactile and sonic connections between the interior dwelling spaces and natural environment surrounding the building. The home's programmatic layout was derived directly from the natural features found within the site. For example, dappled light that filters through the site's trees amplifies the haptic quality of gathering spaces and the sound quality of the adjacent babbling brook brings tranquility and calm to spaces used for reading and writing.

The internal gathering areas were positioned in a way that connected them to the outdoor garden. In this way, the threshold between interior and exterior or natural and artificial was diminished and the natural beauty of the site was brought into the building both visually and sonically.

The vaulted living and kitchen areas nest between the two vertically clad bedrooms. The horizontal and vertical cladding on the exterior elevations articulate this interior dwelling relationship. Given the compact nature of this house, the efficient use of space, strategic control of natural light, and expansive sightlines have the effect of making the space seem more expansive. The great room opens to the east with a window wall that faces the lake, flooding the dining and living areas with warm natural lighting in the morning. High west-facing clerestory windows wash the vaulted ceiling in the afternoon, providing additional lighting for the kitchen and washroom. A central hallway runs the full length of the house to maximize the efficiency of space and movement, like a spine that organizes the building's interior. The resulting interior environment is bright and offers a neutral gallery-like atmosphere that directs focus and frames the exterior views. The end result is an efficient and compact space that is outwardly focused to nature.

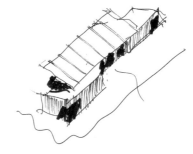

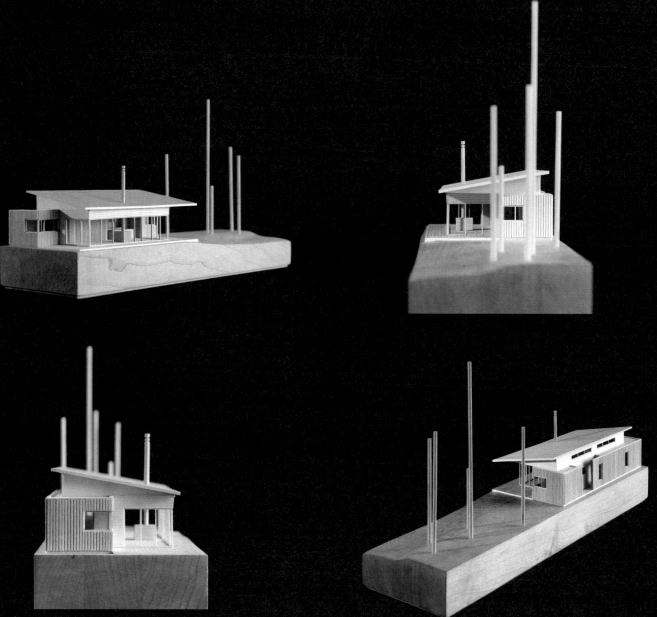

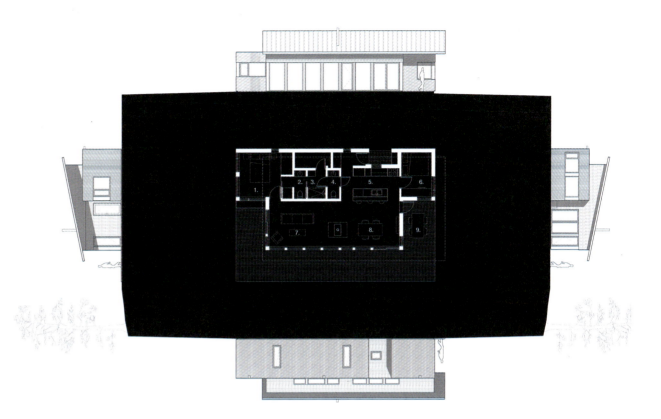

Plan

1. Main Bedroom
2. Main Bathroom
3. Shower
4. Powder Room
5. Kitchen
6. Guest Bedroom
7. Living Room
8. Dining Room
9. Outdoor Dining Room

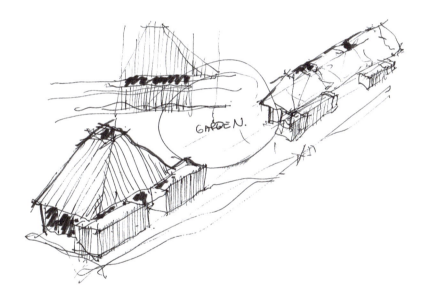

Essay

by Brian Carter

February 3, 2024

The Workshop is the Craftsman's Home[1]

The Back Bay Studio is situated on a rocky outcrop on the Chebucto Peninsula at the eastern edge of Canada – an area defined by forests and the ocean, tiny fishing communities along rugged coastlines and vast swathes of land that make up a Provincial Wilderness Area.

Designed by Peter Braithwaite it was the place where he established his practice in 2014. The development on this site references his particular way of working. Committed to the craft of making as a fundamental part of design it is a practice that recalls Homo Faber – a classical idea of "man the maker" advanced in the writings of Hannah Arendt and Richard Sennett. The Back Bay Studio was designed to house the architect and his workshop.

A long and narrow double height volume, the studio provided space where Braithwaite could design, build and live. Living and work spaces were planned in the double height space and high up at one end a loft provided a place to sleep that could also become a conference space. The form of the studio recalls a telescope that here focuses on long views of the forest and the ocean beyond. In addition a continuous strip of windows offers views out across the site. This building also forms a tall wall that hovers above the ground and shelters that site from the elements.

Braithwaite works enthusiastically with wood. However sawdust, paints and sprays created problems within the studio and consequently he designed and built new workshops alongside. Planned within two separate huts they together define a third outdoor workspace.

These new workshops at Terence Bay confound familiar concepts of the type. Unlike the vast top-lit halls and wide spaces housing serried ranks of equipment that focus on efficiency and production and characterize the industrial spaces of the machine age like those in Detroit designed by Albert Kahn, these workshops are modest spaces of work that recall the primitive hut and reference domestic compounds in traditional cultures like those documented by Rudofsky.

However, all seek economy and at Terence Bay each hut is modest. Enclosing 600 and 240 square feet of space planned on one floor and 18ft in height they house woodworking machines with one fitted out for assembly and finishing. And while the buildings are not identical twins they clearly project family resemblances. They also define an outdoor courtyard that serves as a third space where large assemblies can be constructed and prototypes tested.

These huts are simple yet carefully considered. Their eccentric forms have been developed to provide protection from the wind, induce natural ventilation within the workspaces and catch the sun. Walls are opened to provide views out to the landscape, capture daylight and enable access. A stark contrast to the large singular linear block of the studio alongside, these workshops appear as strange tiny objects that suggest flotsam alongside the breakwater wall of the studio.

Each hut is framed using small sections of wood and the light timber framing, wood and metal cladding create another stark contrast with the large sections of engineered lumber and extensive planes of glass that make up the construction system and enclosure of the adjacent studio.

This is a place that references both head and hand and, as Braithwaite readily confirms, "Back Bay joinery shops exhibit the core values of our firm".

[1] *The Craftsman, Richard Sennett, Yale University Press, 2008. Page 53.*

BACK BAY JOINERY SHOPS

Location: Terence Bay, Nova Scotia, Canada

The Back Bay Joinery Shops are located in the firshing community of Terence Bay, Nova Scotia. The shops provide a creative space for our firm to test, develop and construct design ideas. In collaboration with our design team, our skilled carpenters and cabinet makers use these shops to develop architecture models, scale design detail mock-ups, and fabricate much of the furniture and cabinetry that furnish the buildings we create. The programmatic goal of the project was to create spaces that enable a fluid and efficient workflow between design, fabrication, and finishing. By locating the buildings adjacent to the property road, the workshops respect and minimize the footprint on the sensitive coastal environment as well as strategically restricting the movement of larger vehicles on the property. The central location of the shops on the property also aims to minimize the noise emitted to maintain strong relationships with the local community.

The larger workshop provides a dynamic space for carpentry, design and fabrication while the smaller workshop is primarily used for finishing work and storage. The compositional relationship between the two shops and the courtyard creates an interconnected space that handles a diverse range of projects and fabrication techniques. As a result, both structures are formally connected by large garage doors and a spacious gravel courtyard. The intermediary space created between the buildings acts as a multi-use overflow space where shop activities spill outside during the summer months. The strong formal axial relationship between the shops allows a productive assembly system as well as minimizing unnecessary inefficiencies between materials and carpenters.

A simple gable form and humble material palette reflect our firm's dedication to honouring the vernacular forms and material culture of the place in which buildings reside. The shops were entirely built by our firm's carpenters and local tradesmen from the Terence Bay area with the intent to support local businesses and forge strong personal relationships in the surrounding community. The compact and carefully considered design allowed both structures to be built efficiently by a small carpentry team, which in turn drastically reduced the overall cost of construction.

The Back Bay Joinery Shops exhibit all the core values of our firm: a deep appreciation for design, dedication to craftsmanship, and commitment to build projects that fully integrate with the local community. The shops have been instrumental in helping our firm take on a wider range of projects and have created a deeper connection between our design and our construction teams.

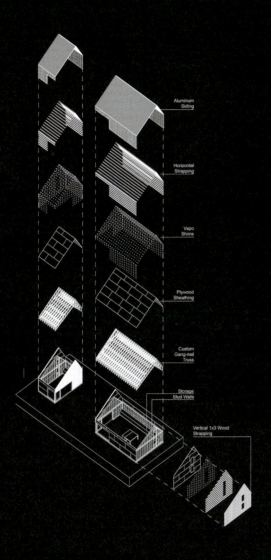

Aluminum
Siding

Horizontal
Strapping

Vapo
Shims

Plywood
Sheathing

Custom
Gang-nail
Truss

Storage
Stud Walls

Vertical 1x3 Wood
Strapping

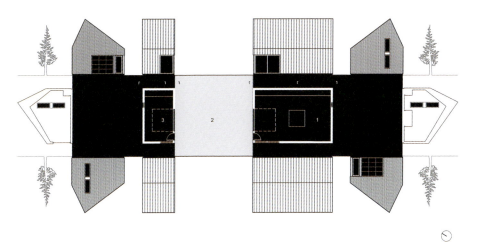

Plan

1. Joinery Workshop
2. Courtyard
3. Finishing Studio

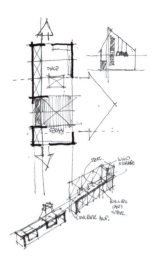

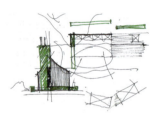

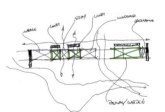

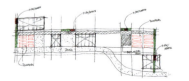

CARIBOU POINT STUDIO /
MEET IN THE MIDDLE HOUSE

The resolution of functional spaces for both work and relaxation maintained an unimpeded physical and visual relationship to the natural environment that drove the fundamental design concept for this project. This dwelling and studio was designed for two artists in the rural Nova Scotian community of Pictou, which is well known for its fishing industry. The elongated linear form stretches along the flat, sweeping natural landscape and creates a harmonious connection between the natural and the constructed. The building acts as a type of aperture for viewing the ever changing seasons and climatic conditions throughout the year along the Nova Scotian coast.

Each end of the project is flanked by a fully tailored studio designed for the specific needs of each artist. Although these separate sectors of the buidling are used to design and create, the occupants come together for daily living, dwelling and gathering activities in the middle of the structure.

Although the program is broken into working and dwelling spaces, the long ribbon-like form of the building acts to unify the spaces through the use of vaulted ceilings and a central hallway that runs the length of the entire building. Adjacent to the great room, the building is penetrated by an exterior breezeway which gives sheltered outdoor space for gathering and engaging with nature.

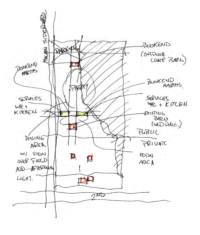

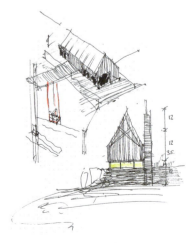

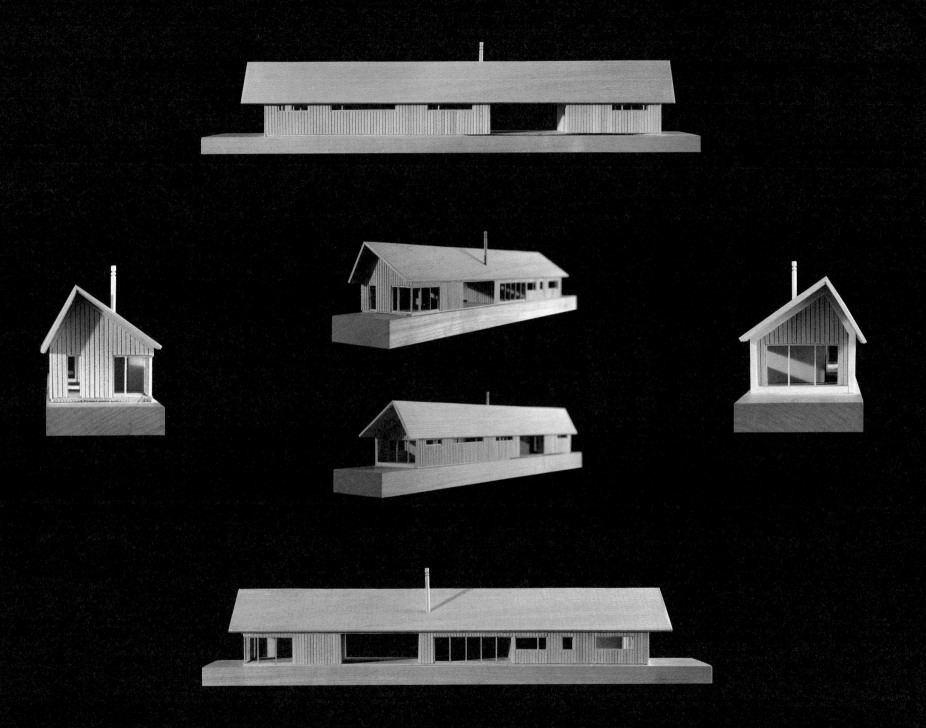

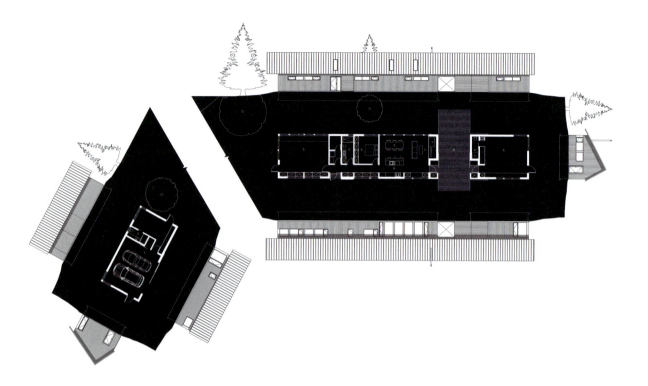

Plan

1. Two Car Garage
2. Bathroom
3. Creative Studios
4. Main Bedroom
5. Dining Room
6. Kitchen
7. Living Room
8. Breezeway

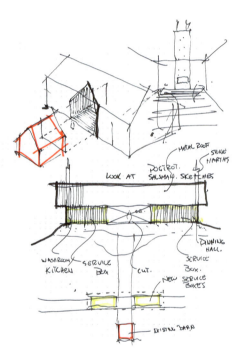

ARMCRESCENT RESIDENCE

Location: Halifax, Nova Scotia, Canada

Located in Halifax's long-established West-End neighborhood, this project represents an architectural exportation into increasing urban density without violating the established urban street fabric proportions or land-use patterns. This residence represents new opportunity for multi-generational or blended family dwelling within one structure rather than breaking down a family unit to accommodate the established archetypes found within the neighborhood.

During the schematic design phase of this project, a strong emphasis was placed on creating diverse and distinct dwelling opportunities that could satisfy a variety of inhabitants' requirements. These included young children in elementary school, teenage children at university, active working adults, as well as accommodating opportunities for extended family and guest visits. The resulting physical form created a living environment that was sympathetic to the urban context while establishing an alternative model for single unit dwellings within Halifax's downtown core.

Driven by a desire to have this residence represent something unique and bold while also remaining respectful of the local material culture, the exterior materials were selected to include a variety of familiar contextual types such as horizontal wood cladding and standing seal metal. However, the exterior colour palette was strongly restricted to highlight the playful interpretation of the traditional east-coast saltbox building form. We felt this also presented the building as a type of silhouette on the landscape rather than confusing or diluting the strong formal qualities with excessive colours and textures.

Similarly, the interior design strategy for the residence was developed to express a contemporary approach using familiar vernacular material. The building's interior celebrated a diverse material palette of wood, steel, and concrete that are cohesively held together with careful detailing and thoughtful connections.

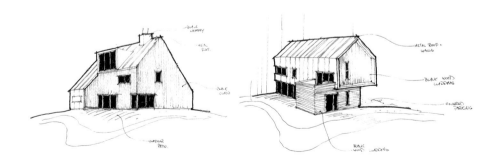

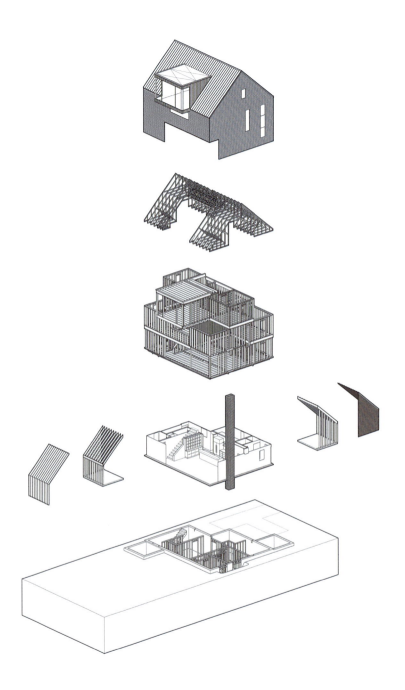

Exploded Axonometric

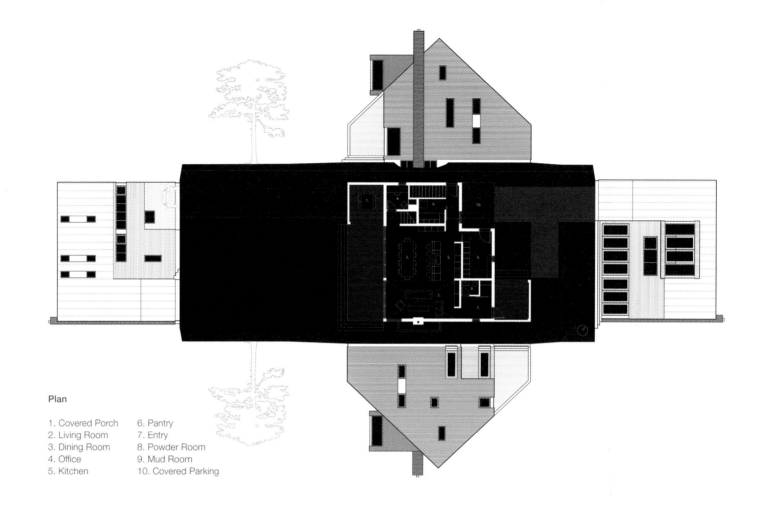

Plan

1. Covered Porch
2. Living Room
3. Dining Room
4. Office
5. Kitchen
6. Pantry
7. Entry
8. Powder Room
9. Mud Room
10. Covered Parking

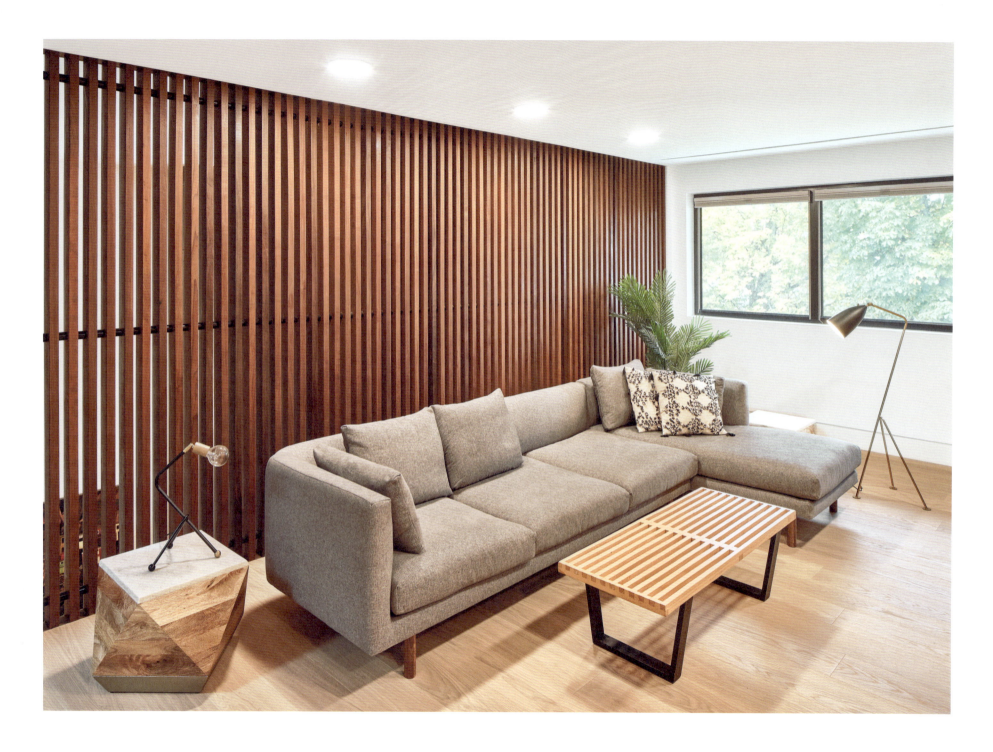

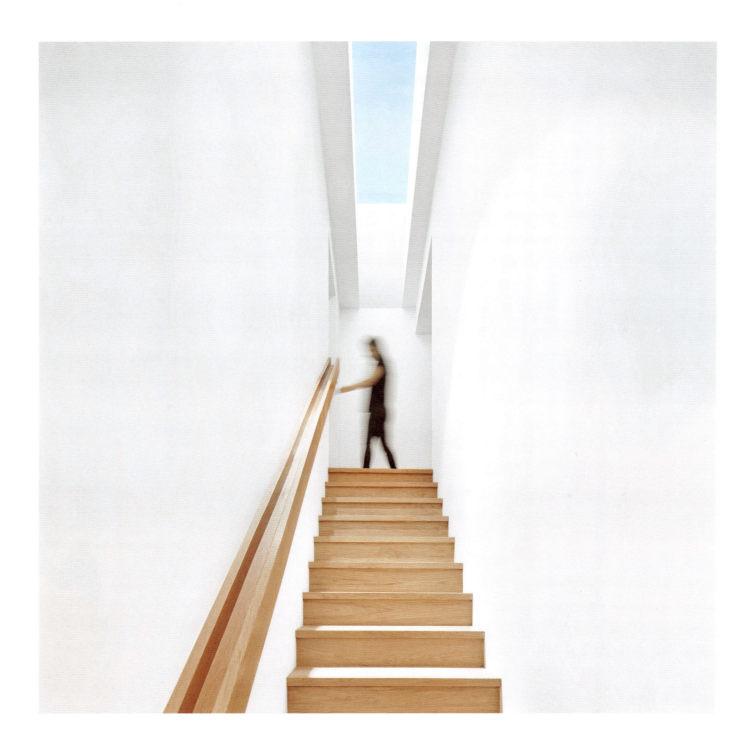

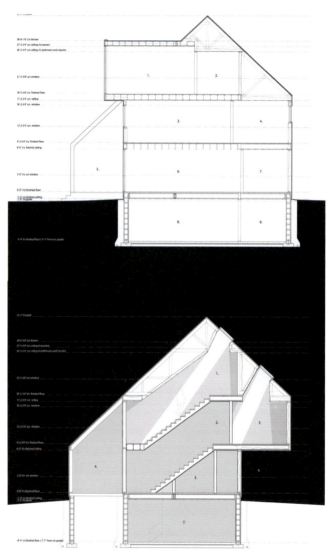

Section A

1. Master Bedroom
2. Master Bathroom
3. Kid's Living Room
4. Bedroom
5. Covered Porch
6. Great Room
7. Mud Room
8. Recreation Room
9. Storage

Section B

1. Stair to Master Bedroom
2. Stair to Kid's Living Room
3. Bedroom
4. Covered Porch
5. Pantry
6. Covered Parking
7. Recreation Room

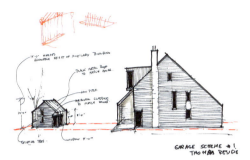

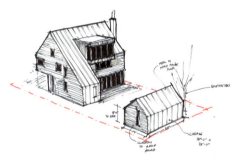

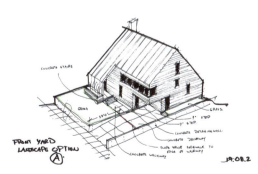

ELM HOUSE

Location: Halifax, Nova Scotia, Canada

Located in the desirable Tupper School District of Halifax, this house displayed great potential for the young family who had recently purchased the property. Over the decades, this residence had been the subject of a number of poorly executed renovations. To address this, our team stripped the layers of vinyl and wood cladding back to the original ship-lap sheathing. We then rebuilt the exterior of the home with the intention of creating a project that was sustainable in both design and construction practices.

Our primary design intention was to create functional responses to the existing building, by utilizing contemporary design and construction practices without disrespecting the historic Halifax neighborhood in which the house resided. This was accomplished by maintaining the original gable form of the building and adding thoughtfully designed additions that refined the functional use of the structure. A new entry porch was added that provided the home owners with a panoramic view of the beautiful tree-lined street. This entry porch also contains a new eight foot wide staircase that encourages and facilitates gatherings of neighbors on summer evenings.

Similarly, the rear of the house was redesigned around ideas of gathering and practical storage. Because the family are keen gardeners, a wood clad storage volume was added to the rear of the building to house garden tools, as well the children's bicycles and toys. Through the use of integrated doors, that were clad in the same material as the walls, this storage volume also acted as a functional visual and audio bookend that helps minimize any disturbance to the neighbors.

The existing main building volume was cladded in horizontal clapboard whereas the new front and rear accent volumes were cladded in locally sourced rough sawn Hemlock. We feel the result is a strikingly contemporary residence with a material palette and formal response that shows respect to the neighborhood in which it resides.

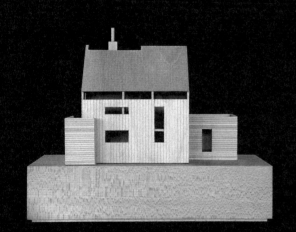

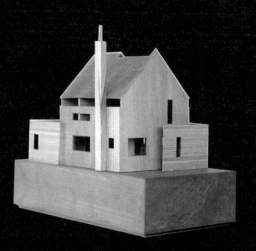

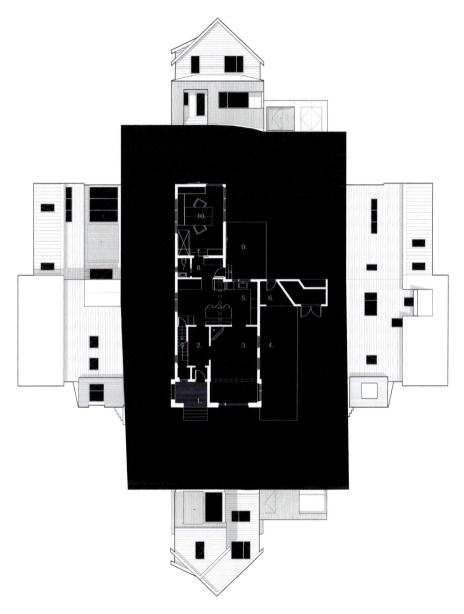

Plan

1. Covered Porch
2. Entry Hall
3. Living Room
4. Paved Driveway
5. Kitchen
6. Covered Backyard Entrance
7. Powder Room
8. Mudroom
9. Outdoor Patio
10. Study Room

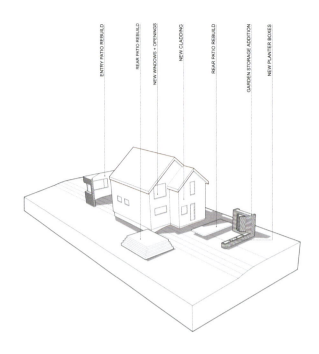

ENTRY PATIO REBUILD
REAR PATIO REBUILD
NEW WINDOWS + OPENINGS
NEW CLADDING
REAR PATIO REBUILD
GARDEN STORAGE ADDITION
NEW PLANTER BOXES

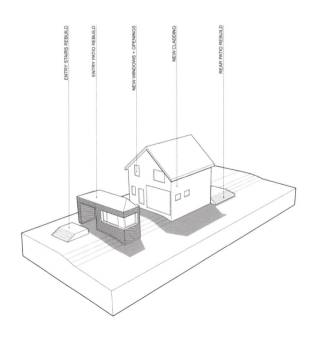

ENTRY STAIRS REBUILD
ENTRY PATIO REBUILD
NEW WINDOWS + OPENINGS
NEW CLADDING
REAR PATIO REBUILD

LAMBKILL RIDGE COTTAGE

Location: Terence Bay, Nova Scotia, Canada

The affectionate moniker of Lambkill Ridge is derived from the common name for a local plant, Sheep Laurel, which can be found in abundance along the barren lands of Terence Bay, Nova Scotia. Designed as a getaway for a four-person family of nature enthusiasts, the architecture features two nearly identical volumes mirrored along a long, narrow boardwalk that connects the access road to the winding nature trails beyond. Hoisted up off the forest floor and thrust into the tree canopy, the intention was to situate the user prominently in the natural environment, provide breathtaking views over the barren lands and out to the ocean from the loft spaces within, and encourage the natural landscape to continue to thrive throughout. The long ascent up the two-tiered stairwell and along the boardwalk provides views to the entrance of a subtle trailhead that is framed by the two darkened volumes.

The first volume that you encounter upon your climb is the sleeping pavilion, where you will find the mechanical closet boasting fully sustainable equipment, a full bath, and sleeping loft above. The second volume, also known as the living pavilion, houses a white-oak-clad kitchenette, the main living space with a wood burning stove and a guest sleeping loft above. Designed to be largely off-grid, key features include a window designed to maximize both thermal heat gain, as well as passive ventilation to help regulate temperatures in all months of the year, an incinerating toilet, and a rainwater collection and filtration system.

While the exterior volumes sit starkly in the landscape, the interior materiality draws upon local resources and adds prominent design features to this modest project. Locally sourced, rough-hewn hemlock is showcased while highlighting typical light-timber framing practices found in the region. As the structures are "outsulated" (insulation on the outside of the framing), black-metal electrical conduits along with other black-metal features are strewn throughout adding a level of industrialism which juxtaposes the raw nature of the hemlock.

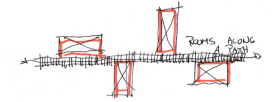

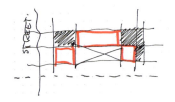

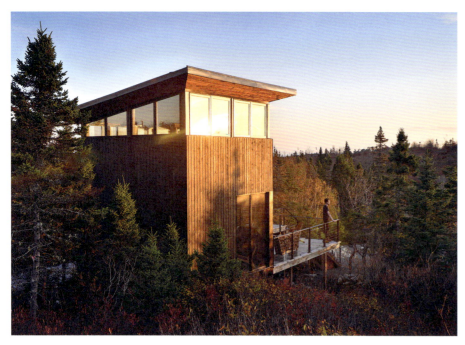

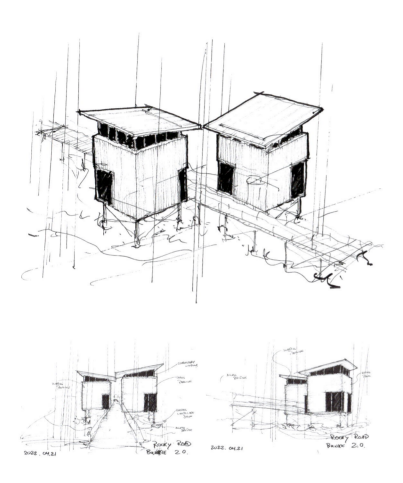

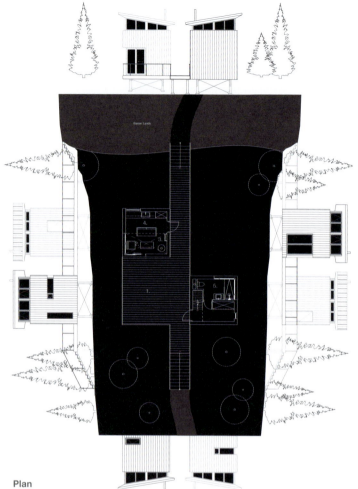

Plan

1. Deck
2. Living Room
3. Wood Stove
4. Kitchenette
5. Bathroom

A-FRAME

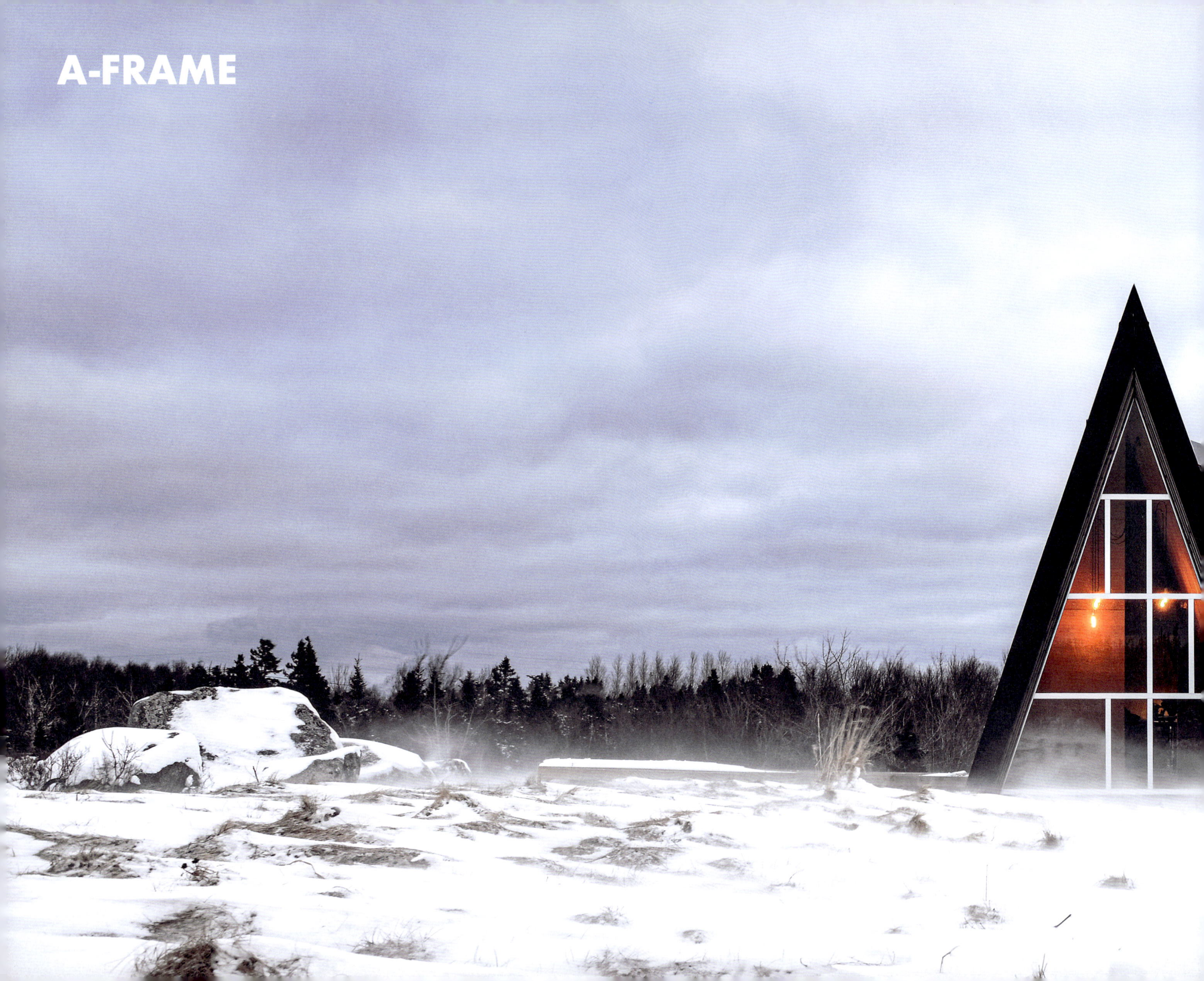

Location: Terence Bay, Nova Scotia, Canada

As a personal and experimental project, the Back Bay A-Frame began during a two week design-build course with Dalhousie School of Architecture students. Initially imagined as a public boat house, the A-Frame gradually developed into a private residence while navigating the building permit process following the student's involvement.

Much of the design work and development of this building occurred through the act of building, rather than as a design exercise that was removed from the site features. As a result the form of this building naturally and sympathetically rises from a existing pocket in the bedrock then cracks its plan to orient itself inline with the sun and ocean views. Without a typical 'client,' and the usual hinderance of timelines, this project has provided our team with an opportunity to explore new methods of building such as pre-fabricated panelized cladding systems, custom-built aluminum window walls, a concrete bathtub that was poured in place, and an exploratory structural system.

The interior of the building provides a warm and comforting environment with white oak clad walls and polished concrete floors throughout. The great room is divided into three programmatic sections for gathering, eating, and cooking with each space having it's own elevations within the room. The viewpoints from each space are designed to connect specific environmental features around the building with each unique aspect of dwelling.

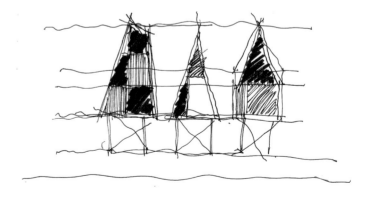

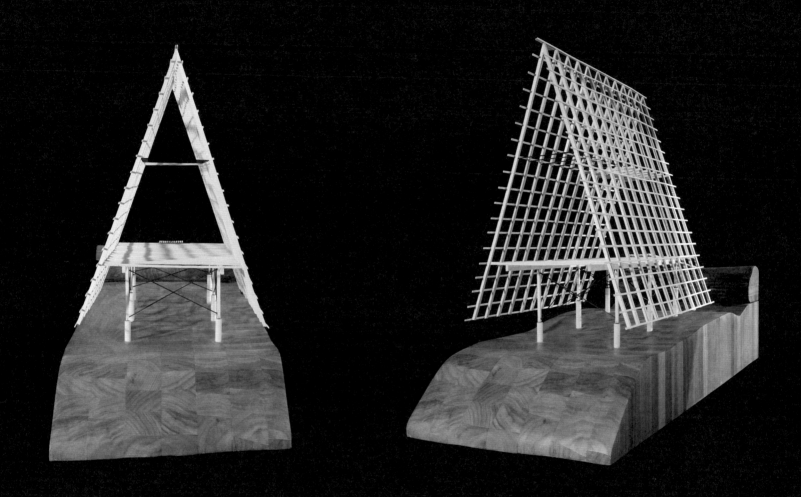

Plan

1. Bathroom
2. Entry
3. Kitchen
4. Dining Room
5. Living Room

MARTINIQUE BEACH HOUSE

Location: East Petpeswick, Nova Scotia, Canada

Situated in a beautiful coastal region of Nova Scotia, only minutes from the longest sandy surf beaches in the province, this project was designed around the notion of "aging in place." The design brief became particularly challenging given that accessing the ocean view and sun above the existing tree canopy was also of extreme importance to the homeowners. The resulting form was a three story home connected vertically by a concrete circulation core that contained both stairs and a one person elevator. The program of the dwelling was divided vertically with the bottom floor containing services and an entry mudroom, a second floor dedicated to sleeping and the upper level providing the primary living and gathering spaces accented by a breathtaking view out to the ocean.

Extreme sensitivity toward the natural landscape was a primary driver during both the design and construction of this project. Primary focus was placed on retaining as many trees and indigenous shrubs as possible throughout the development of the project.

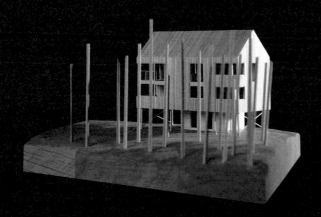

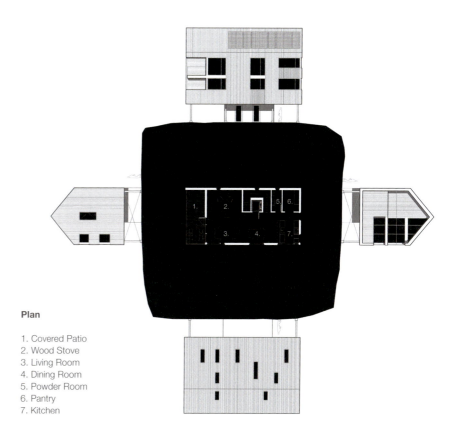

Plan

1. Covered Patio
2. Wood Stove
3. Living Room
4. Dining Room
5. Powder Room
6. Pantry
7. Kitchen

Essay

by Peter Braithwaite

Natural Forces: Crafting a Nova Scotian Identity

Geographically Nova Scotia resembles a peninsula that has been thrust from the eastern shore of Canada into the North Atlantic Ocean. Apart from a narrow isthmus that connects the province with the rest of North America, it is surrounded by the sea. The shore meanders in and out of the rocky bays and boulder covered hillsides that define the distinctly rugged coastline. To the north is the Gulf of St. Lawrence, to the east and south is the Atlantic Ocean and to the west is the Bay of Fundy, known for a unique hydrographical phenomenon resulting in the world's highest tidal range.

Most communities in Nova Scotia reside close to the sea. They find refuge in the sheltered inlets and protected harbours that stipple the shoreline. Long stretches of windswept forests show the signs of the harsh hurricane winds that frequent this part of Canada. Climate patterns based on latitude and elevation are muted in Nova Scotia due to the interaction of the cold Labrador Current and the warm Gulf Stream. In this way, to understand the weather of this place you must also understand the ocean. The rhythmic advancement and retreat of the tide defines when to work, when to play, and when to hunker down and take shelter. The imprint of the ocean can be found in almost every aspect of eastern Canadian culture but nowhere is this more apparent than within the architecture.

Built primarily from stunted trees battered by coastal wind and salt spray, the traditional structures of Nova Scotia appear so light that they could blow away. The houses, fishing sheds, and wharfs that are found clustered along the sea's edge seem to cling to the rocks in an intimate dialogue with their surroundings. Ingenuity, thrift, and endurance has defined a cultural understanding of how to build in this place and these values are reflective of our firm's approach to design and craft. Understanding the subtle relationship between the sea, the climate and the material culture remains a guiding principle within our work. As much an act of observation as an exercise in creation, we aspire to interpret the natural dynamics of each site prior to undertaking the design process. Working within a frugal and humble context, our work manifests itself in simple forms, humble material palettes, and non-ostentatious detailing. Undertaking both the architecture and the construction of our projects, we challenge the notion that design is strictly a precursor to the act of construction. We perceive building as the medium through which design ideas are expressed.

Projects Under Construction

TWILIGHT HOUSE

Location: Terence Bay, Nova Scotia, Canada

Perched on a cliff edge in Terence Bay, Nova Scotia, this house captures panoramic views of the ocean and the rugged East Coast landscape. Although this site displays striking, uninterrupted views of Back Bay and the open ocean beyond, the dwelling's program was not designed around this visual focal point alone. The project owners are deeply engaged with meditation and tranquility, so it was equally important to them to engage the calm natural "refuge" environment to the north of the site as it was to engage with the sweeping view of the ocean to the south. In this way a clear programmatic distinction between "prospect" and "refuge" was created.

For these reasons, the house was designed as two adjoining forms connected by a wood-clad link. Each volume was designed to have its own unique elevation and view of the landscape as well as representing distinct internal environments. The public or "prospect" living volume overlooks the expansive ocean views and includes the dwelling's gathering spaces that include the living room, dining room, library, and kitchen. Alternatively, the private or "refuge" volume looks down onto a small calm pond that is fed by a babbling stream. This private volume contains areas of solitude or refuge which include the bedrooms, large bath areas, a mediation room, and an outdoor spa that all endeavour to enhance a sense of relaxation and encourage a connection to the natural environment and landscape.

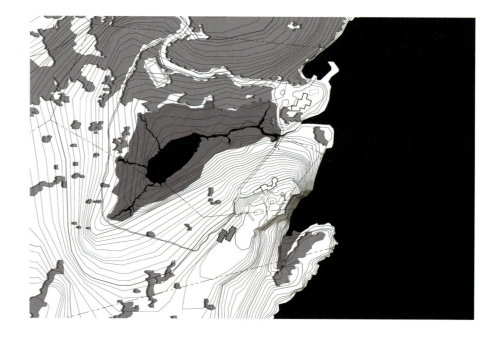

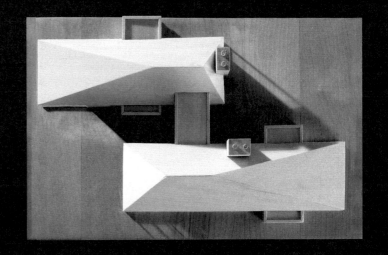

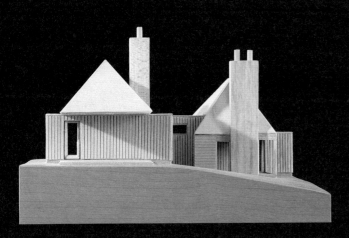

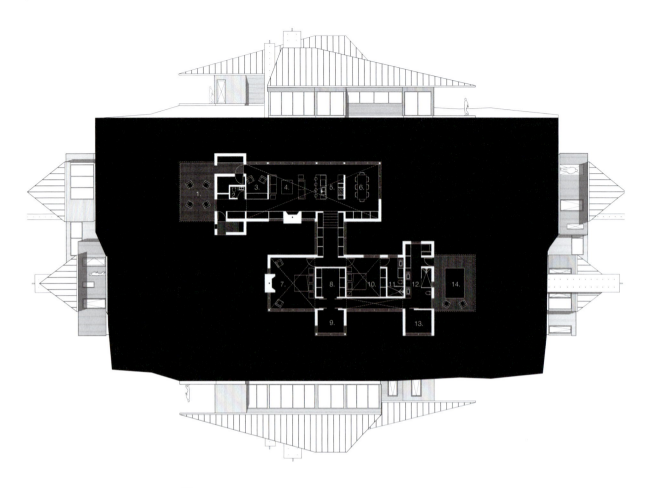

Plan

1. Covered Patio
2. Powder Room
3. Library
4. Living Room
5. Kitchen
6. Dining Room
7. Main Bedroom
8. Main Closet
9. Meditation Room
10. Guest Bedroom
11. Guest Bathroom
12. Main Bathroom
13. Exercise Room
14. Pool

NARROWS RESIDENCE

Situated along a rocky shoreline that overlooks Back Bay in the rural fishing town Terence Bay, Nova Scotia, the Narrows Residence was positioned to minimize the building's impact on the site's sensitive coastal environment while strategically enhancing access to the extraordinary sight lines out to the Atlantic Ocean. Capturing a panoramic view of the rugged coastal terrain while also considering the potential for passive cross ventilation informed the positioning of the building's large opening and exterior patios.

The material selection for the residence was based on local vernacular precedents. The upper living volume is proposed to be clad entirely of locally sourced and locally milled Hemlock boards to enhance the tectonic nature of the light timber framed structure. Alternatively, the lower core volume presents a stereotomic approach to structure and enclosure where the concrete walls will be scribed and fastened to the high bedrock which is customary in the region.

The steel bridge stretching west from the main living volume is intended to extend the program, both physically and conceptually, beyond the dwelling enclosure and connect the inhabitants with the rugged boulder shoreline found along the Atlantic coast. The intent is to enhance the sensory experience of the building by providing an armature through which one will find greater access to the sounds, smells, and views of the ocean and coastline. The physical construction of this bridge is intended to resemble the long span piers, structures and docks that are found scattered along the shoreline of Atlantic Canada.

A simple gable form and a humble material palette reflects a desire to honour the vernacular forms and material culture of the place in which buildings reside. The Narrows Residence exhibits all the core values of our firm: a deep appreciation for design ingenuity, dedication to craftsmanship, and an unwavering commitment to build projects that fully integrate with the local community.

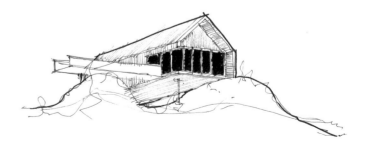

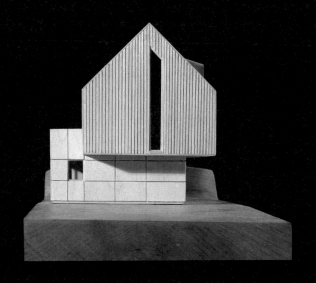

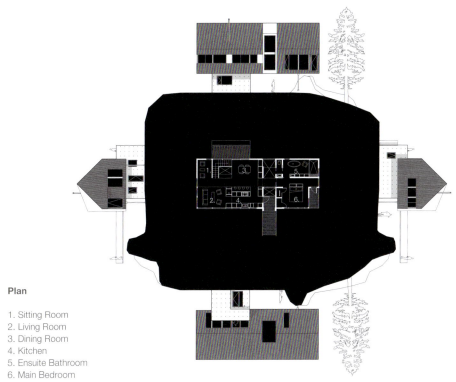

Plan

1. Sitting Room
2. Living Room
3. Dining Room
4. Kitchen
5. Ensuite Bathroom
6. Main Bedroom

B-FRAME

Location: Kings County, Nova Scotia, Canada

The B-Frame is the largest of the Attic Dwelling models and offers much more than the fundamentals of the rural life. The project was conceived as a two bedroom residence with a double height gathering space that extends into a large outdoor viewing platform. The essence of the project is a floating A-Frame form that intersects a monolithic concrete volume, creating a unique response to typology and site.

The building is accessed through the stereotomic vertical circulation core that also acts as the structural anchor for the tectonic A-Frame structure and allows the extension of the structure beyond the structural bays below. Simplification of the A-Frame form not only promotes the use of a economical and efficient construction typology but also aids in providing protection from the heavy rains and large snowfall that are customary in the region.

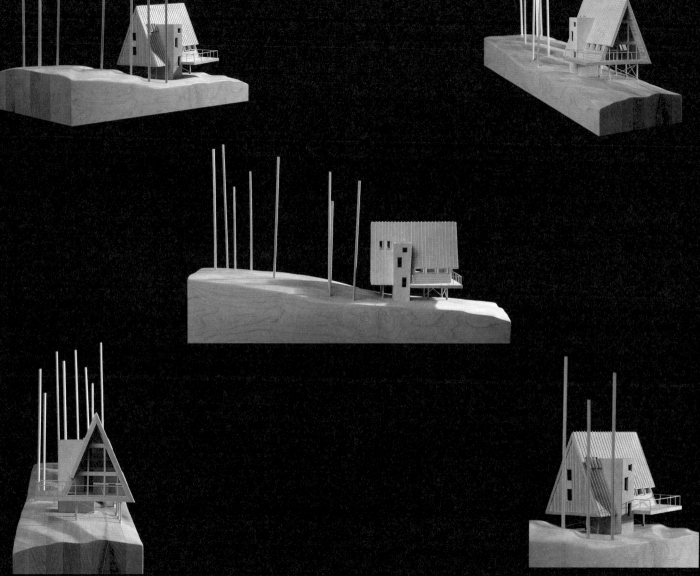

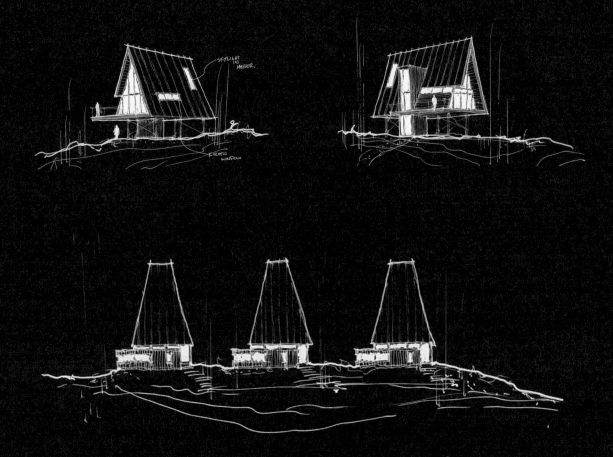

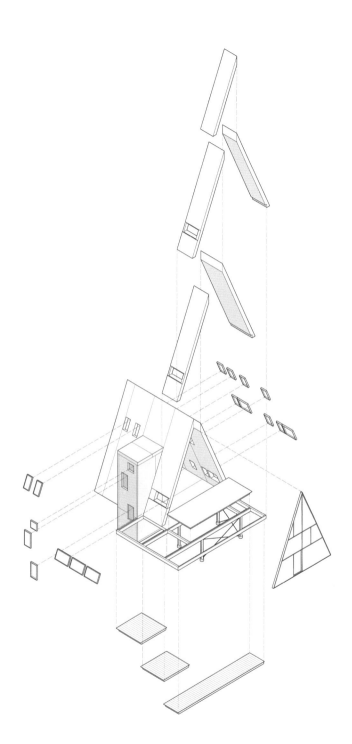

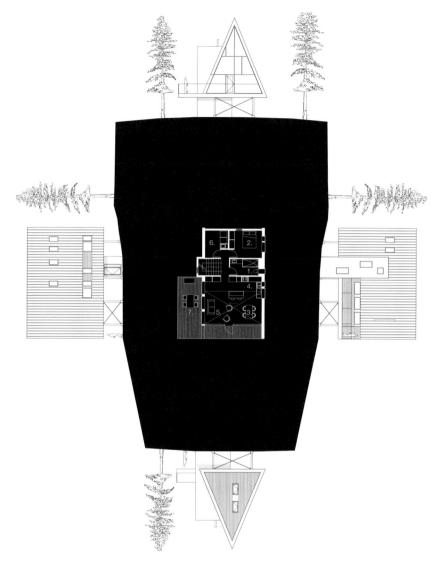

Plan

1. Bathroom
2. Main Bedroom
3. Dining Room
4. Kitchen
5. Living Room
6. Machanical/Laundry
7. Patio

GABLE ENDS COTTAGE

Similar to the fishing huts that pepper the eastern Canadian coastlines, the Gable Ends Cottage serves as a reminder that elegance can be found within the simplest of forms. With severe, coastal weather events becoming seemingly more frequent, lifting this structure up off the landscape ensures comfortable refuge during adverse coastal weather events while also providing its inhabitants with stunning views over the rugged eastern Canadian landscape.

This building's efficient rigid frame design allows easy manipulation of the building's size and complexity based on individual client requirements and spatial desires without the need for extensive structural redesigns. The single span nature of the building's joists and rafters mimic the surrounding vernacular fishing buildings that demonstrate great efficiency and economy in their design.

Wrapped almost entirely with fully seamed standing seam metal, this building is designed to handle the harsh horizontal wind, rain, and snow that is customary in Atlantic Canada.

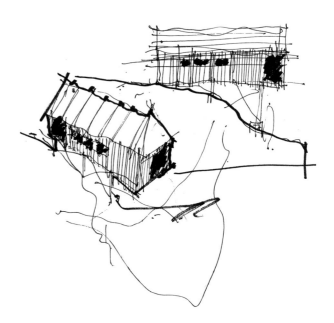

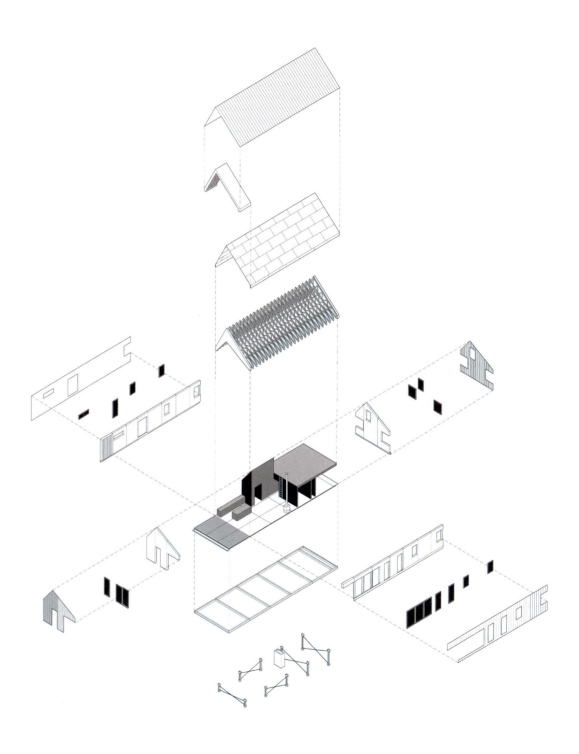

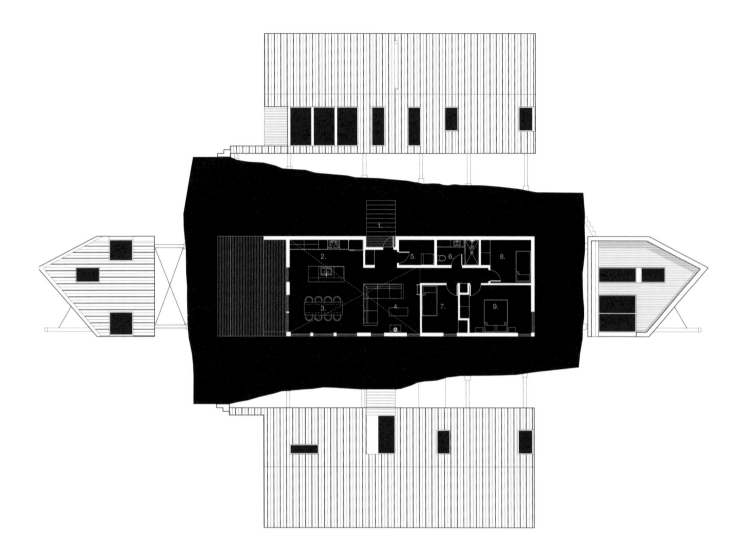

Plan

1. Entry
2. Kitchen
3. Dining Room
4. Living Room
5. Mechanical/Laundry
6. Bathroom
7. Bedroom 3
8. Bedroom 2
9. Main Bedroom

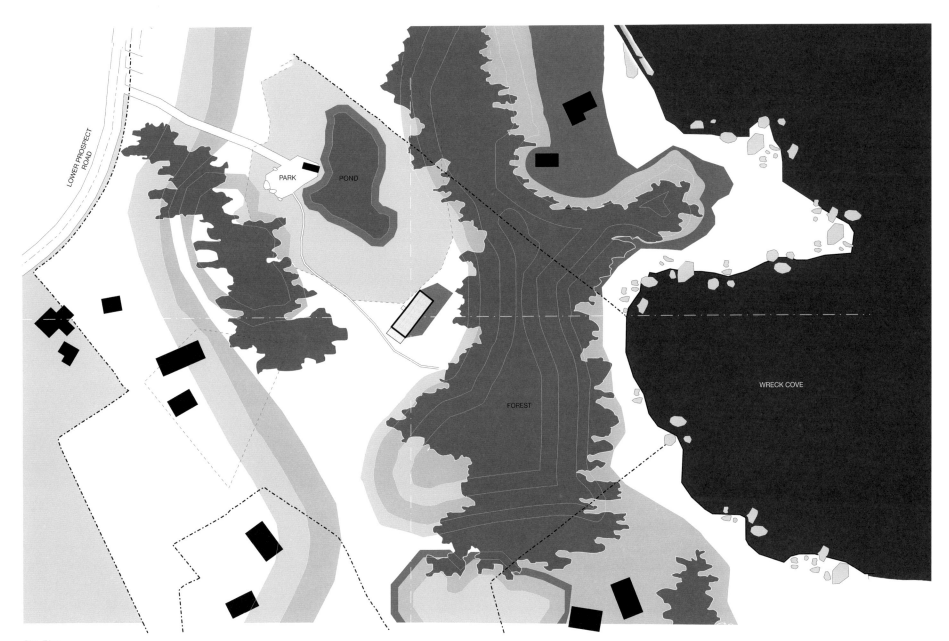

LOWER PROSPECT ROAD

PARK

POND

FOREST

WRECK COVE

Site Plan

ROCKY ROCK CABIN

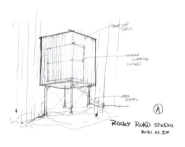

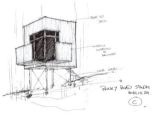

Location: Terence Bay, Nova Scotia, Canada

Providing the smallest footprint of the Attic Dwellings models, the Rocky Cabin is intended to minimize the disruption to the natural environment while providing panoramic views of the coastline and rolling landscape found in Atlantic Canada. The compact nature of this structure provides great flexibility given it can fit within almost any landscape while also providing the essentials of comfortable dwelling. Upon entering this structure occupants are met with double height windows that wrap the corner and extends ones view out to the landscape making this humble structure seem much larger. Above the central gathering spaces is a sleeping loft that can be customized with a spiral or linear stair based not the occupants desire. The loft if intended to be a place of quite refuge and focus ones view out to strategically placed framed views.

The simple light timber frame structural design allows great flexibility in fenestration and orientation on a site which provides great opportunities to tailor this structure to a variety of different sites and locations.

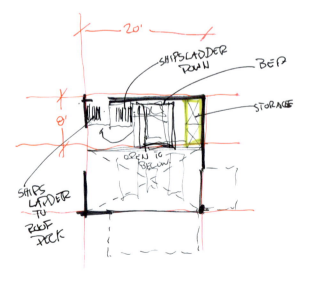

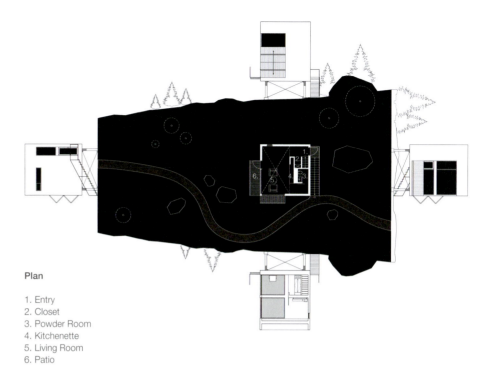

Plan

1. Entry
2. Closet
3. Powder Room
4. Kitchenette
5. Living Room
6. Patio

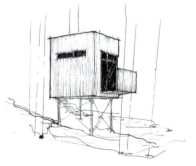

ATTIC LOFTS

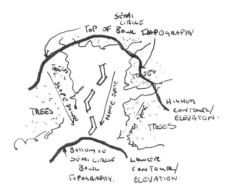

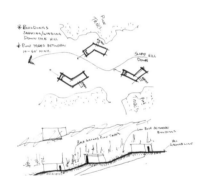

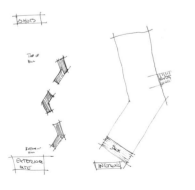

Location: Terence Bay, Nova Scotia, Canada

As the form and structure of this building coincide, the repetitions of internal structural bays offer simple spatial divisions that help to delineate and guide the internal program. The cranked floor plan creates hierarchy and separation between the two resulting spaces that include a large public gathering spaces that is intended to be immersed in natural light while smaller more intimate spaces lay beyond that are intended to be tucked into naturally sheltered areas within the landscape. The tall roof structure, that inspired this structures name, allows an elevated refuge loft and a contrasting view of the expansive landscape from a higher datum.

Being the one Attic Dwellings structure that is not lifted up off the landscape, this building is intended to scribe and nestle within the naturally undulating rocky landscape found throughout Nova Scotia. The result is a building focussed on a synergy with the natural world and ecological features of the site enabling the occupants to experience a calming, tranquil relationship with the natural world. The warm and minimal nature of the buildings finishes aim to encourage occupants to look beyond the architecture and instead engage with the present landscape.

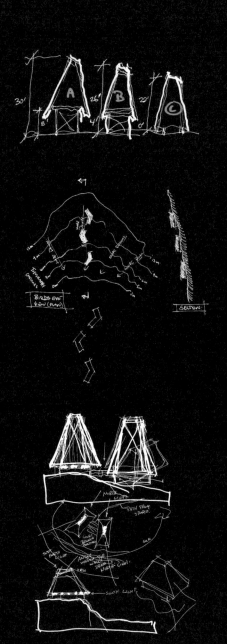

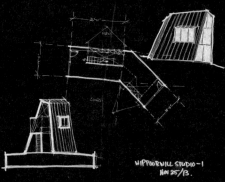

WIPPOORWILL STUDIO-1
NOV 25/13.

WIPPOORWILL STUDIO-1
NOV 25/13.

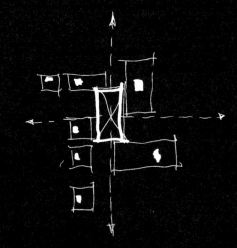

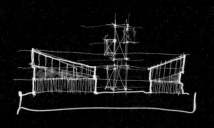

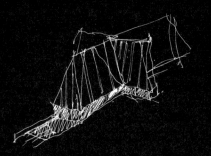

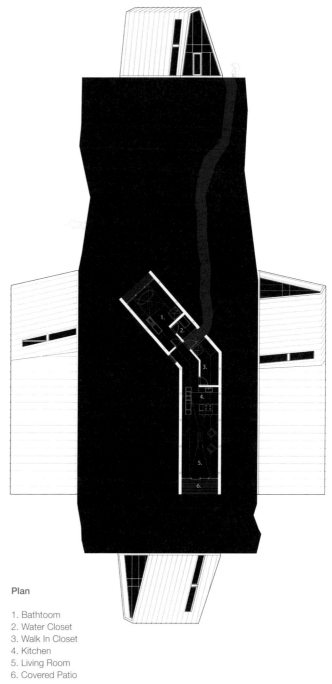

Plan

1. Bathtoom
2. Water Closet
3. Walk In Closet
4. Kitchen
5. Living Room
6. Covered Patio

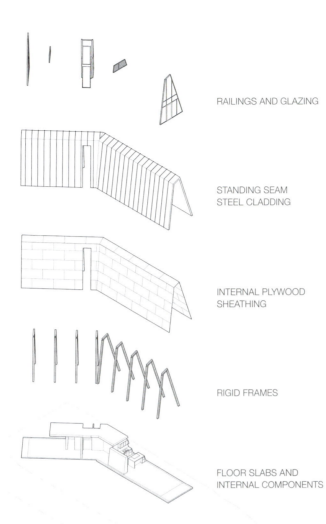

RAILINGS AND GLAZING

STANDING SEAM
STEEL CLADDING

INTERNAL PLYWOOD
SHEATHING

RIGID FRAMES

FLOOR SLABS AND
INTERNAL COMPONENTS

BLACK POINT RESIDENCE

Location: Black Point, Nova Scotia, Canada

This expansive residence was designed for a retired couple looking to design a home that could host their extended family for holidays and large family gatherings. Located along Northumberland Strait in Black Point, Nova Scotia, the building's form is comprised of three distinct geometric volumes which each comprise specific programmatic functions. The two gable structures have specific programmatic functions in that one is dedicated to shared living and gathering spaces while the other is dedicated to sleeping and bathing. The third rectilinear volume intersects and skewers both gables and contains the building's circulation and services spaces. Each volume is rotated at the intersection of their axes to optimize their views and sun exposure.

The building's interior puts its structure on display with exposed steel portal frames and rough-sawn rafters. The interior materiality accentuates the building's volumetric and programmatic organization. To accommodate large family gatherings, the program includes an extra-large kitchen and dining table, a variety of seating areas, and multiple spaces dedicated to their grandchildren. At the culmination of the circulation axis, a fireplace anchors the building's social activity within a dramatic cantilever. The site's landscaping is graded to create expansive walk-outs for the basement and main floor, creating secondary outdoor entertainment spaces and connecting the interior and exterior programs.

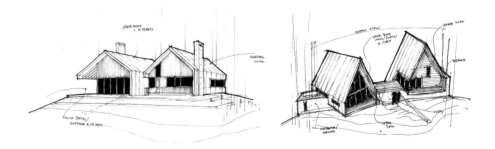

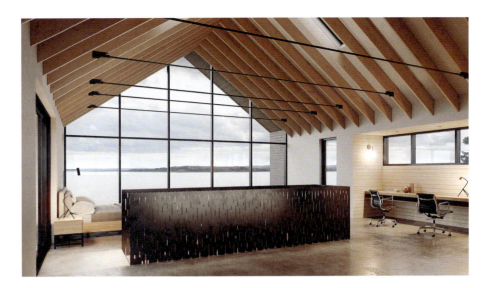

Plan

1. Entryway
2. Kitchen
3. Dining Room
4. Family Room
5. Living Room
6. Patio
7. Main Bedroom
8. Work Space
9. Walk-In Closet
10. Main Bathroom

ARMSTRONG ISLAND

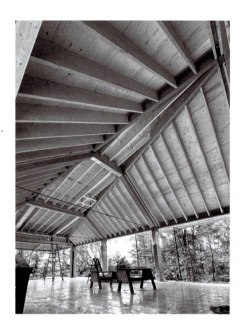

Location: North Kawartha, Ontario, Canada

Designed as a off grid, net zero family relaxation destination, this project presented the opportunity for a young Toronto based family to rekindle nostalgic childhood memories by designing a cottage on the lake they has spent their summer months as a child. Given the isolated nature of the site, our team knew the project would be logistically complex. The commissioning of barges, the construction of docks capable of rising and falling with the seasonal lake water level changes, and organizing the transportation of heavy machinery over the frozen ice during the winter months kept our design team engaged and anxiously awaiting whatever new obstacle might reveal itself as the project progressed through construction.

Born out of a desire to spend time within the natural environemnt with their two growing children, the project owners placed environmental concerns at the forefront of the project design and construction practices. The resulting built volumes engage with the natural environment while remaining light on the land and sesitive to the native ecosystem. The two pavilions that make up this dwelling, sleeping and living, were placed on stilts within natural occurring clearings on the island. In this way the building appears to hover within the tree canopy while allowing the natural landscape to slip below.

This elevated nature of the building volumes was structurally accomplished by fastening steel wide flange columns to the native bedrock below. . This construction strategy drastically decreased the amount of concrete required for the project which was beneficial given the isolated nature of the project and the toxic qualities concrete might have been introduced into the fertile topsoil found on the island. The remainder of the building's superstructure was designed as a 'kit of parts' where structural member were selected with the intention of maximizing their innate structural properties and their ease of transporation to site. What resulted was wood and steel beams, lam beam rigid frames, wood and steel hip members and wood rafters that could be transported to site by barge then easily assembles on site with steel plates and bolts.

Every effort has been made throughout the design and construction of this project to ensure the building systems were sustainable, highly efficiency and contained low life cycle imbeded energy.

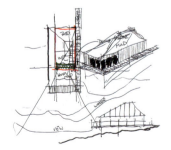
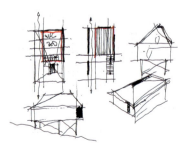

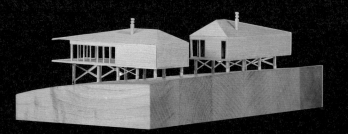

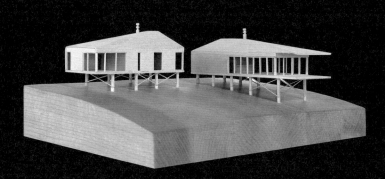

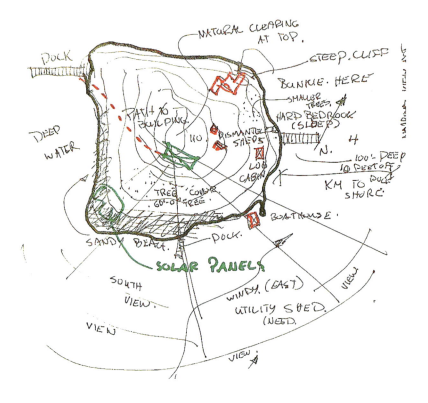

Main Pavilion

Guest Pavilion

Boat House

1. Entryway
2. Mechanical Room
3. Pantry
4. Bathroom
5. Kitchen
6. Dining Room
7. Living Room
8. Covered Patio
9. Connecting Hallway
10. Outdoor Patio
11. Bedroom 3
12. Bedroom 2
13. Main Bathroom
14. Main Bedroom
15. Covered Porch
16. Entry
17. Bedroom
18. Common Room
19. Bathroom
20. Covered Patio
21. Entry
22. Boat Storage
23. Covered Patio

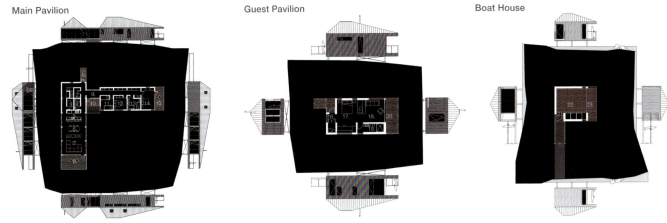

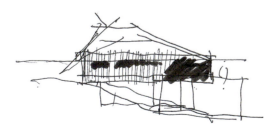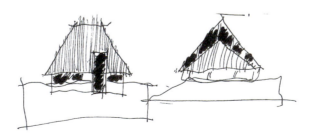

Interview

James McCown
& Peter Braithwaite

Peter Braithwaite I grew up in Kingsville – a small town in south western Ontario. My parents had studied zoology and veterinary science and that certainly shaped my childhood. I was also interested in building things and built models before constructing larger things – working with my family to build small decks, shelters, and sheds. Working on these projects took me to a local lumber yard and I began to work there. After graduating from high school I worked in that same lumber yard for a year while figuring out what to do with my life.

In the lumber yard I first worked as a forklift driver. Later I drove a flat deck truck and delivered materials. It was good introduction to building materials, what they were used for and the people who used them.

James McCown Did you study woodworking?

PB In Ontario at that time there were wood working classes in high schools. However the curriculum was organised in such a way that you were either in school with an intention to be a tradesperson or an academic. Students had to choose early and college education tended to be geared towards the trades while university education was focused on more intellectual pursuits. Given my family background I wanted to pursue an academic career. However the wood shop was also a place that I gravitated to.

In the workshop there were some predetermined things that you had to build – I recall a clock for example. Subsequently we got to design things that we made. I remember building a box but also being more interested in the actual joinery than in specific objects. Making dovetail joints was a particular interest.

Working with my hands was always enjoyable. I had a strong sense of perfectionism. I've continuously tried to balance it with productivity.

JM What happened after high school?

PB I followed the path of natural science and pursued a degree in biology at the University of British Columbia in Vancouver. During my studies there I also worked part-time as a carpenter. I became more and more interested in designing and building. I began studying fine arts and design and this led me to Dalhousie University in Halifax where I applied to study architecture. I enrolled there in 2008 and since then the School of Architecture has become a second home. After receiving my degree I was invited to teach and we regularly employ students from Dalhousie's coop program. I enjoy working with students.

JM Did living and studying in Canada – one of the largest countries in the world and one with almost unfathomable amounts of forests – make wood important for you and influence your practice there?

PB Wood is a renewable resource and consequently it makes sense to develop ways of using it. Engineered lumber – CLT (cross-laminated timber) and LVL (laminated

veneered lumber) is increasingly used in the design and construction globally. However the supply chain in in Eastern Canada is fragile so we haven't adopted it perhaps as we could have. A few years ago a fellow from the West coast of Canada worked in our practice. He was skilled in the use of engineered lumber but surprised to discover how little we had adopted it.

Wood is often a viable alternative to reinforced concrete and from an environmental point of view it is, of course, a much better alternative.

JM I recall that Frank Lloyd Wright defined wood as "the most intimate of all materials, man likes his association with it, likes its fell under his hand, sympathetic to his touch and his eye."

PB Those characteristics are important for me – wood has strength, a tactile quality and can bring warmth into a building.

Atlantic Canada has a long tradition rooted in the use of light timber frame construction. It is intertwined with the culture of this place. But we have small, spindly trees so builders in Eastern Canada have had to figure out ways to build using 2" X 4" sections and explore ways of stacking and connecting to enclose space. This frugal approach to the use of wood in buildings in our region is also influenced by boat building – an activity that has a long history in the Maritimes.

I have always been interested in building with wood and the act of making. Carpenters are fundamental people in our design team.

JM Who are your architectural heroes?

PB I have been influenced by Scandinavian design and its sense of simplicity. Having travelled there and spent time in Oslo the work there is really inspiring. However I am not so sure about architectural heroes. There are definitely valuable lessons that can be learned from notable architects across time but that being said, my particular interest in architecture has always been more firmly rooted in materials and their use, in material cultures and the ways that buildings can respond to climate. The most valuable lessons that I have learned have come through making. It continues to shape my views of architecture – perhaps far more than the influence of any particular architects.

Glen Murcutt's sensibility to the natural landscape is inspiring. It seems to me that it is more important to consider form in the context of the natural environment rather than adopting a more domineering stance. My life as part of a family dedicated to the natural sciences has shaped my view of architecture.

James Cutler is another architect who considers the siting of buildings carefully. Finding an appropriate synergy between built form and natural landscape is clearly evident in his work. It inspires me.

And Juahni Pallasmaa's book *The Eye of the Skin* is very influential for me. Its emphasis on tactile qualities and the characteristics of materials make it a constant reference.

JM Has travel influenced your approach to architecture?

PB I have had the opportunity to travel to number of places within Europe, Scandinavia, and Africa.

Those travels made me more aware of the weather, land and the weathering of buildings. Greater awareness of nature and climatic differences has made me consider the impact of time and place relative to architecture. This has influenced the forms we consider, construction details and the way we work. It has also prompted us to consider particular materials and how they age – cedar shingles and Corten for example.

JM Your work is primarily residential. Do you have aspirations for the future?

PB We enjoy designing houses and each is very different from the other. There are also ideas that we would like to pursue that will likely be advanced through larger and more civic commissions. Time will tell.

I don't have all the answers. The journey is just beginning for me but I am excited by prospects for the future. I constantly remind myself that architecture is a marathon not a sprint!

January 21, 2024, BC

Project Credits

Back Bay Studio
Architecture + Design: Peter Braithwaite
Structural: Andrea Doncaster Engineering
Construction: Peter Braithwaite, Ben Biggley, Devin Harper, Jeff Shaw,
Ryan McNeill, Tom Lutes, David Burlock
Photographs: Julian Parkinson, Peter Braithwaite, Jason Petersson, Riaz Oozeer
Drawings + Models: Peter Braithwaite, Matt Gillingham

The Sandbox
Architecture + Design: Peter Braithwaite, Jody Miller, Abby Lawson, Lucien Landry
Structural: Corbo Inc.
Construction: GOMA Construction, Pro Construction, Elevation Enterprises
Visualization: Yurii Suhov
Photographs: Ema Peter
Drawings + Models: Lucien Landry

Seabright Residence
Architecture + Design: Peter Braithwaite, Matt Gillingham, Jody Miller
Structural: Andrea Doncaster Engineering
Construction: Peter Braithwaite Studio Ltd.
Photographs: Julian Parkinson, Peter Braithwaite
Drawings + Models: Peter Braithwaite, Matt Gillingham

Back Bay Joinery Shops
Architecture + Design: Peter Braithwaite
Structural: Andrea Doncaster Engineering
Construction: Peter Braithwaite, Ryan McNeill, Tom Lutes, Devin Harper,
Ben Biggley, John Marshall
Photographs: Peter Braithwaite, Julian Parkinson, Jason Petersson
Drawings + Models: Matt Gillingham

Caribou Point Studio / Meet in The Middle House
Architecture + Design: Peter Braithwaite, Matt Gillingham, Jody Miller
Structural: Andrea Doncaster Engineering
Construction: Peter Braithwaite Studio Ltd.
Visualization: Yurii Suhov
Photographs: Peter Braithwaite, Ema Peter
Drawings + Models: Peter Braithwaite, Matt Gillingham

Armcrescent Residence
Architecture + Design: Peter Braithwaite, Matt Gillingham, Jody Miller
Structural: Andrea Doncaster Engineering
Construction: Peter Braithwaite Studio Ltd.
Photographs: Peter Braithwaite, Julian Parkinson
Drawings + Models: Peter Braithwaite, Cait Stairs, Matt Gillingham

Elm House
Architecture + Design: Peter Braithwaite, Matt Gillingham
Structural: Andrea Doncaster Engineering
Construction: Peter Braithwaite, Devin Harper, Ryan McNeill
Photographs: Peter Braithwaite, Julian Parkinson
Drawings + Models: Peter Braithwaite, Matt Gillingham

Lambkill Ridge Cottage
Architecture + Design: Peter Braithwaite, Odin Paas, Lucien Landry
Structural: Andrea Doncaster Engineering
Construction: Peter Braithwaite Studio Ltd.
Photographs: Peter Braithwaite
Drawings + Models: Jam Basilio, Lucien Landry, Odin Paas

A-Frame
Architecture + Design: Peter Braithwaite,
Odin Paas, Lucien Landry
Structural: Andrea Doncaster Engineering
Construction: Peter Braithwaite Studio Ltd.
Photographs: Peter Braithwaite
Drawings + Models: Peter Braithwaite,
Lucien Landry, Kyle Cheeseman

Martinique Beach House
Architecture + Design: Peter Braithwaite
Structural: Andrea Doncaster Engineering
Construction: Peter Braithwaite Studio Ltd.
Visualization: Yurii Suhov
Photographs: Peter Braithwaite
Drawings + Models: Peter Braithwaite,
Lucien Landry, Kyle Cheeseman

Twilight House
Architecture + Design: Peter Braithwaite, Matt Gillingham, Jody Miller
Structural: Blackwell Structural Engineering
Visualization: Yurii Suhov
Drawings + Models: Peter Braithwaite, Matt Gillingham

Narrows Residence
Architecture + Design: Peter Braithwaite,
Devin Harper, John Marshall
Structural: Andrea Doncaster Engineering
Visualization: Yurii Suhov
Drawings + Models: Cait Stairs, Peter Braithwaite, Lucien Landry

B-Frame
Architecture + Design: Peter Braithwaite, Lucien Landry, Abby Lawson
Structural: Andrea Doncaster Engineering
Visualization: Yurii Suhov
Drawings + Models: Lucien Landry, Abby Lawson, Odin Paas, Jam Basilio

Gable Ends Cottage
Architecture + Design: Peter Braithwaite, Jody Miller, Lucien Landry
Visualization: Yurii Suhov
Drawings + Models: Lucien Landry, Odin Paas, Keegan Gray

Rocky Rock Cabin
Architecture + Design: Peter Braithwaite, Olivia Raposo,
Peter Boeckeler, Odin Paas, Lucien Landry
Structural: Andrea Doncaster Engineering
Visualization: Yurii Suhov
Drawings + Models: Olivia Raposo, Odin Paas

Attic Lofts
Architecture + Design: Peter Braithwaite, Matt Gillingham
Structural: Andrea Doncaster Engineering
Visualization: Yurii Suhov, Ryan Nelson
Drawings + Models: Cait Stairs, Matt Gillingham, Kyle Cheeseman, Clair Robertson

Black Point Residence
Architecture + Design: Peter Braithwaite, Jody Miller, Matt Gillingham
Structural: Andrea Doncaster Engineering
Visualization: Yurii Suhov
Drawings + Models: Peter Braithwaite, Jody Miller

Mason's Point Residence
Architecture + Design: Peter Braithwaite, John Marshall
Structural: Andrea Doncaster Engineering
Visualization: Yurii Suhov
Drawings + Models: Matt Gillingham, David Burlock, Cait Stairs

Armstrong Island
Architecture + Design: Peter Braithwaite, Matt Gillingham, Jody Miller
Structural: Blackwell Structural Engineering
Construction: Beacon Construction
Visualization: Yurii Suhov
Photographs: Peter Braithwaite
Drawings + Models: Matt Gillingham, Peter Braithwaite, Keegan Gray

Selected Bibliography

2024
Staff. "The Sandbox." Restless Living Magazine, January 5, 2024.

2023
Bernard, Grace. "These Are Dwell's Most Popular Homes of 2023." Dwell, December 2023.
Luco, Andreas. "The Sandbox / Peter Braithwaite Studio." ArchDaily, December 1, 2023.
Betsky, Aaron. Nova Scotia's new vernacular: Peter Braithwaite creates strong form, November 16, 2023.
Mazzucco, Lucy. "Peter Braithwaite Wins Ronald J. Thom Award for Early Design Achievement." Canadian Architect, July 4, 2023.
"Archinect Celebrates Canada Day by Highlighting 15 Architecture Firms That Are Defining the Future of Canadian Architecture." Archinect, July 1, 2023.
"Architect of the Month." Enki Magazine, June 2, 2023.
Staff, Sharp. "Master Builder." Sharp Magazine, May 2, 2023.
Sweet, Elizabeth. "Foul Weather Is No Match for This Boxy New Brunswick Home-or the Steel Stair Wrapped around It." Dwell, February 2023.
Zaharia, Elisa. "The Sandbox, a Wooden Home in Canada." Elle Decor, January 27, 2023.
ArchiloversCom. "The Sandbox: Peter Braithwaite Studio." Archilovers, 2023.

2022
Gendall, John. "Home of the Week: The Sandbox by Peter Braithwaite Studio." NUVO, November 6, 2022.
Stathaki, Ellie. "This Boxy House on the Shores of Canada Celebrates Its Site and Makers." wallpaper.com, November 3, 2022.
Pintos, Paula. "Caribou Point Studio / Peter Braithwaite Studio." ArchDaily, November 2, 2022.
Valentina, Bianca. "Armcrescent Residence / Peter Braithwaite Studio." ArchDaily, April 9, 2022.
Hitchcock, Beth. "Highlighting the Country's Best Architecture, Interiors and Housewares in 2022." The Globe and Mail, January 2022.
Mastine-Frost, Justin. "This Is Not Your Typical East Coast Canadian Architecture." Sharp Magazine, January 11, 2022.

2021
Lam, Elsa. "Twenty + Change: Emerging Talent - Peter Braithwaite Studio." Canadian Architect, August 9, 2021.
Caballero, Pilar. "Seabright Residence / Peter Braithwaite Studio." ArchDaily, February 22, 2021.

Hannah, Jessie. *Small structures of Nova Scotia: Spaces of solitude, necessity, and simplicity*. Halifax, NS: Nimbus Publishing, 2021. Back Bay Studio and Seabright Residence included in book.
Hermanson, Marissa. "This Sun-Soaked Cabin in the Canadian Wilderness Is a Breath of Fresh Air." Dwell, January 14, 2021.

2020
Wood, Jennifer. "Structured Plans." EDIT Magazine, Spring 2020.
The Leukemia & Lymphoma Society of Canada. "Meet the Winners." Visionaries of the Year, 2020.

2019
Halls, Luke. "Canada-based architect Peter Braithwaite selected for Wallpaper* Architect's Directory 2019, June 14, 2019.

2018
Caballero, Pilar. "Back Bay Studio / Peter Braithwaite Studio." ArchDaily, October 10, 2018.
Caballero, Pilar. "Terence Bay Joinery Shop / Peter Braithwaite Studio." ArchDaily, October 7, 2018.
Atwood, Hal. "First Look: Brightwood Brewery's Sunny Gathering Place." The Coast Halifax, August 23, 2018.
Hague, Matthew. "Nova Scotia Architect's Home Studio Is a DIY Beauty." The Globe and Mail, July 31, 2018.
Fontana, Kaitlin. "The Watch That Ends the Night Named Best New Bar in Canada." EnRoute Magazine, July 2018.

2017
Atwood, Hal. "First Look: Inside the Watch That Ends the Night's Cool Canadiana." The Coast Halifax, November 2, 2017.
Mullin, Morgan. "Black Magic on Elm Street." The Coast Halifax, April 6, 2017.

2016
The Chronicle Herald. Making The Old New Again, December 2016.
Leiva, Sabrina. "Elm House / Peter Braithwaite Studio." ArchDaily, December 16, 2016.
Rojas, Cristobal. "South End Residence / Peter Braithwaite Studio." ArchDaily, May 6, 2016.
Parkinson, Julian. "Peter Braithwaite / the Architecture, the Design, the Studio." Format Films, April 2016.

Professional Awards

RAIC Emerging Architectural Practice Award, 2024.

Canadian Council for the Arts - Ronald J. Thom Award for Early Design Achievement, 2023.

Dwell Magazine, Most Popular Houses of 2023, Sandbox, 2023.

Archilovers, Best Project 2023, Sandbox, 2023.

American Institute of Architects (AIA) Canada Council, Award of Excellence, Caribou Point Studio, 2023.

American Institute of Architects (AIA) Canada Council, Award of Merit, Gable Ends Cottage, 2023.

Archinect - 15 Architecture Firms That Are Defining the Future of Canadian Architecture, 2023.

Architizer A+ Awards - Honouring the World's Best Architecture and Spaces - Special Mention - The Sandbox, 2023.

Wallpaper* Magazine's Architects' Directory 2019 - Top 20 of the world's most promising practices, 2019.

Canadian Architect and Twenty + Change - Top 20 emerging practices in Canada, 2021.

Globe and Mail Designing Canada – Country's Best Architecture, 2022.

Lieutenant Governor's Award - Award of Merit, 2018.

EnRoute Magazine - Canada's Best New Bars 2018- Awarded national first place, 2018.

The Architectural League of New York - Young Architects Award (Finalist), 2020.

Atlantic WoodWORKS! Award - Back Bay Studio - Hybrid Building, 2022.

Canadian Co-Op Design Office of the Year - Awarded by Dalhousie University, 2018.

Man of the Year – Leukemia & Lymphoma Society of Canada, 2020.

Canadian Co-Op Design Office of the Year (Nomination), 2022.

Halifax Mayor's Prize in Architecture, 2018.

Academic Awards

Killiam Doctoral Scholarship (Killiam-D) - Dalhousie University, 2022.

Nova Scotia Graduate Scholarship (NSGS-Doctorial) - Dalhousie University, 2022.

Canadian Co-op Design Office of the Year - Nominated - Dalhousie University, 2022.

Royal Architectural Institute Student Medal - Highest Academic Standing, 2013.

President's Award - Dalhousie University, 2022.

Canadian Co-op Design Office of the Year - Awarded by Dalhousie University, 2018.

Harry Kitz Fund - Dalhousie University, 2019.

Royal Architectural Institute Honour Roll, 2013.

Rosetti Scholarship in Architecture, 2011.

Faculty of Graduate Studies Scholarship, 2010.

Peter Braithwaite NSAA, OAA, MRAIC

Peter is the owner and operator of Peter Braithwaite Studio. Since its establishment in 2014, the firm has gained recognition as a leading design firm both nationally and internationally. Prior to pursuing architecture at Dalhousie University in 2008, Peter worked as a carpenter and a cabinet maker. These experiences are evident in his approach to design and construction. His interest in exploring the relationship of climatic factors to construction assemblies and material properties is demonstrated in an unwavering dedication to craft and climate appropriate detailing. Peter feels that true sustainability is found in well-crafted buildings that do not require early replacement and that thoughtful programmatic considerations should result in physical forms that enhance both the natural and the built environment.

Following the completion of a Master of Architecture in 2012, Peter received the Royal Architectural Institute of Canada Student Medal for achieving the highest level of academic excellence in his graduating class. Peter was also awarded a Rosetti Travel Scholarship to conduct studies pertaining to his thesis that explored the relationship between built environments and the natural world. During his graduate studies Peter worked for MacKay Lyons Sweetapple Architects and later took on the position of project manager at Omar Gandhi Architect where he completed his professional architectural internship.

Throughout years of practice, Peter's interest in ecological systems and how they relate to the built environment has grown. In 2021 Peter was awarded a Killiam Doctoral Scholarship to complete PhD studies within Interdisciplinary Studies department at Dalhousie University that explores collaborative design approaches between architects and natural scientists. Peter is also completing a Doctor of Design at University of Calgary School of Architecture, Planning, and Landscape that explores refined construction logistics that diminish habitat fragmentation and encourage greater ecological connectivity within our built environments.

Since 2015 Peter has been a dedicated educator at the Dalhousie School of Architecture in Halifax, Nova Scotia. He has taught two design studios on an annual basis and currently holds the position of Adjunct Instructor. Peter is also a mentor to architectural interns, acts as thesis advisor to graduate students, and employs architectural work-term students at the high school, undergraduate, and graduate level.

Peter Braithwaite Studio

Lucien Landry
associate + intern architect

Olivia Raposo
designer

Abby Lawson
project manager + intern architect

Jam Basilio
designer + carpenter

Colin Reid
carpenter

Peter Braithwaite Studio, a dynamic architecture firm based in Halifax, Nova Scotia, thrives on redefining the essence of "value" in every project. Founded by Peter Braithwaite in 2014, the studio seamlessly integrates architecture design and construction, ensuring a delicate balance between quality and cost.

Working primarily in Nova Scotia, Canada, where projects often grapple with limited budgets and resources, the team tackles the challenge head-on, pursuing innovative ways to infuse "value" without relying on costly materials or intricate connections. This vision materializes through creative applications of vernacular assemblies, and humble material palettes, transforming ordinary elements into captivating sensory experiences and spatial qualities. The results become forms that respect the natural landscape, forging new paths within Atlantic Canadian architecture.

Dedicated to low-impact and sustainable practices, the team believes authentic "value" lies in creating structures that withstand the test of time. This commitment entails meticulous attention to user satisfaction and the delivery of projects with enduring qualities. In the spirit of an old adage, the team embraces the philosophy that "we are too poor to afford cheap," emphasizing the lasting impact of well-crafted, enduring designs.

At the heart of the success lies a team of passionate and highly skilled architects, designers, and carpenters. Committed to design excellence and the highest craftsmanship standards, they play a pivotal role in realizing the architectural vision. The fusion of creativity and craftsmanship enables the team to produce environmentally and culturally sustainable buildings, enriching the communities in which the structures reside.

Peter Braithwaite Studio represents the collaboration of ambitious individuals sharing a common interest in the intersection of design and construction. Rejecting the notion of these disciplines as separate entities, the team views building as the medium through which design ideas come to life. Each project becomes an exercise in both design and construction, fostering a streamlined creation process that eliminates adversarial relationships between designer and builder.

This approach not only enhances project timelines but also contributes to cost-effectiveness by reducing administrative overheads. The studio's reputation for successful project delivery extends beyond residential and commercial ventures, showcasing excellence in cabinetry and furniture design. Their portfolio reflects a consistent dedication to design excellence and the highest standards of craftsmanship, establishing Peter Braithwaite Studio as a beacon of innovation and reliability in the architecture and construction community.

Contributors

Brian Carter

Brian Carter, a registered architect, worked in practice with Arup in Lodnon prior to his appointment as Chair of Architecture at the University of Michigan. He subsequently served as Dean of the School of Architecture and Planning at the University at Buffalo. The author of books on architecture and design he has curated international exhibitions of work by Peter Rice, Albert Kahn, Eero Saarinen and Aires Mateus. Brian Carter is currently Professor of Architecture at the University at Buffalo.

Yurii Suhov

Yurii Suhov is an architectural and product visualization artist with more than 15 years of experience in the field. Yurii was born and raised in Riga, Latvia, where his early years were spent accompanying his architect father to construction sites, instilling a profound appreciation for the field. After graduating from high school, Yurii embarked on architectural studies. However, in 2009, due to the Great Recession, he decided to broaden his horizons and relocated to Toronto, Canada, where he spent three years working in sales.

Upon returning home, Yurii realized his true passion lies in bringing architectural drawings to life through imagery. In 2013, he decided to shift his focus exclusively to architectural visualization. He constantly explores various disciplines to broaden his artistic pursuits, integrating 3D work with photography and digital matte painting. Influenced by a background in architecture and interior design and a keen interest in graphic design, photography, and music, his practice approaches each project with a natural curiosity and a beginner's mind. Yurii and Peter initiated their collaboration in 2018 following a short email exchange. They have continued to collaborate, successfully completing more than a dozen projects. Among these projects, the most notable, in Yurii's opinion, is the Attic Cottages. Thanks to the wonders of modern technology, Yurii's practice is rooted in the places he finds himself. Most recently, he spent two years living, working, and surfing by the Atlantic Ocean in Portugal.

Aaron Betsky

Aaron Betsky is a Professor at Virginia Tech. Previously, he was President of the School of Architecture at Taliesin. A critic of art, architecture, and design, Mr. Betsky is the author of over twenty books on those subjects. He writes a once-weekly blog for architectmagazine. com, Beyond Buildings. Trained as an architect and in the humanities at Yale University, Mr. Betsky has served as the Director of the Cincinnati Art Museum (2006-2014) and the Netherlands Architecture Institute (2001-2006), as well as Curator of Architecture and Design at the San Francisco Museum of Modern Art (1995-2001). In 2008, he also directed the 11th Venice International Biennale of Architecture. His latest books are Fifty Lessons from Frank Lloyd Wright (2021), Making It Modern (2019) and Architecture Matters (2019). His Anarchitecture: The Monster Leviathan will be published by The MIT Press in 2023.

Ema Peter

Ema Peter is an award-winning Canadian photographer considered to be among the top architecture photographers in the world. Based in Vancouver, British Columbia, Canada, she is known for taking a photojournalist approach to capture the relationship between built forms and the people who live and work within them. She has photographed buildings and interiors across North America, designed by such notable architects as BIG, Kengo Kuma, KPF, Luis Vidal Architects and many more. Born in Sofia, Bulgaria, Peter's interest in photography began at six when she received her first camera from her father. He also taught her how to develop negative film in the family's kitchen.

She regularly travelled with her father, who was a cameraman on film sets, and oftentimes slept in his car full of film gear. Both experiences were formative in developing her observational skills and how to capture light and shadow through a lens. Peter studied photography at the National Academy of Theatre and Film Arts in Sofia, where she earned a Master's Degree in art and applied photography. She discovered her passion for French photographer Henri Cartier-Bresson and his "decisive moment" concept while an intern at the Magnum Photos agency in Paris. Cartier-Bresson has played a significant role in informing Peter's work and her inclusion of human elements within the stark beauty of modernist architecture.

In 2001, she immigrated to Canada and started working for Expedia, shooting luxury hotels worldwide. Later, she began photographing projects by local architects and eventually took on work by leading firms across North America.

Her love for contemporary design stems from "seeing so many drab, grey concrete buildings" in her youth during the Eastern European communist era. "I don't like conventional. I don't like old-fashioned," she has said. "I've always aimed for the future, and I think that comes from the fact that I lived in a very past state, and maybe part of me wants to see the future." Peter's photography has been featured on the covers of over 50 architecture and design publications. In 2023, she was the recipient of the Créatuers Design Award for Best Project Photographer. She has won the Architizer awards, Dezeen awards, Canadian Architect awards and many more.

James McCown

James Moore McCown is a Boston-based architectural journalist who writes for numerous design publications including Metropolis, Architect's Newspaper and AD PRO Architectural Digest. He has collaborated with Oscar Riera Ojeda on several books including the Architecture in Detail series which comprised four volumes: Elements, Materials, Colors and Spaces. McCown studied journalism at Loyola University New Orleans and holds an ALM (Master's Degree) in the history of art and architecture from Harvard University, where his thesis on modern Brazilian architecture received an Honorable Mention, Dean's Award, Best ALM Thesis (2007). He lives in Newton, Massachusetts.

Oscar Riera Ojeda

Oscar Riera Ojeda is an editor and designer based in the US, China, and Argentina. Born in 1966, in Buenos Aires, he moved to the United States in 1990. Since then, he has published over three hundred books, assembling a remarkable body of work notable for its thoroughness of content, timeless character, and sophisticated and innovative craftsmanship. Oscar Riera Ojeda's books have been published by many prestigious publishing houses across the world, including Birkhäuser, Byggförlaget, The Monacelli Press, Gustavo Gili, Thames & Hudson, Rizzoli, Damiani, Page One, ORO editions, Whitney Library of Design, and Taschen. Oscar Riera Ojeda is also the creator of numerous architectural book series, including Ten Houses, Contemporary World Architects, The New American House and The New American Apartment, Architecture in Detail, and Single Building. His work has received many international awards, in-depth reviews, and citations. He is a regular contributor and consultant for several publications in the field. In 2001 Oscar Riera Ojeda founded ORO Editions, a company at which he was responsible for the completion of nearly one hundred titles. In 2008 he established his current publishing venture, Oscar Riera Ojeda Publishers, a firm with fifteen employees and locations across three continents.

Book Credits

Graphic design by Florencia Damilano
Art direction by Oscar Riera Ojeda
Copy editing by Kit Maude

OSCAR RIERA OJEDA
PUBLISHERS

Copyright © 2024 by Oscar Riera Ojeda Publishers Limited
ISBN 978-1-946226-90-7
Published by Oscar Riera Ojeda Publishers Limited
Printed in China

Oscar Riera Ojeda Publishers Limited
Unit 1331, Beverley Commercial Centre,
87-105 Chatham Road South, Tsim Sha Tsui, Kowloon, Hong Kong

Production Offices
Suit 19, Shenyun Road,
Nanshan District, Shenzhen 518055, China

International Customer Service & Editorial Questions: +1-484-502-5400

www.oropublishers.com | www.oscarrieraojeda.com
oscar@oscarrieraojeda.com